THE MANAGER'S DILEMMA

THE MANAGER'S DILEMMA

Balancing the Inverse Equation of
Increasing Demands and
Shrinking Resources

JESSE SOSTRIN

palgrave
macmillan

THE MANAGER'S DILEMMA
Copyright © Jesse Sostrin, 2015.

First published in 2015 by
PALGRAVE MACMILLAN®
in the United States—a division of St. Martin's Press LLC,
175 Fifth Avenue, New York, NY 10010.

Where this book is distributed in the UK, Europe and the rest of the world,
this is by Palgrave Macmillan, a division of Macmillan Publishers Limited,
registered in England, company number 785998, of Houndmills,
Basingstoke, Hampshire RG21 6XS.

Palgrave Macmillan is the global academic imprint of the above companies
and has companies and representatives throughout the world.

Palgrave® and Macmillan® are registered trademarks in the United States,
the United Kingdom, Europe and other countries.

ISBN: 978–1–137–48579–3

Library of Congress Cataloging-in-Publication Data

Sostrin, Jesse.
    The manager's dilemma : balancing the inverse equation of increasing
    demands and shrinking resources / Jesse Sostrin.
        pages cm
    Includes bibliographical references and index.
    ISBN 978–1–137–48579–3 (hardcover : alk. paper)
    1. Executives—Job stress. 2. Management. 3. Problem solving. I. Title.

HF5548.85.S67 2015
658.4'09—dc23   2014048239

A catalogue record of the book is available from the British Library.

Design by Newgen Knowledge Works (P) Ltd., Chennai, India.

First edition: July 2015

10 9 8 7 6 5 4 3 2 1

Printed in the United States of America.

For Sophia: from one author to another!

CONTENTS

FIGURES

TABLES

PREFACE

THIS BOOK WAS BORN OUT OF THE frustration and confusion I felt as a manager who was struggling to get everything done while feeling overmatched by the volume, pace, and intensity of the challenges I faced. Despite my continued advancement through the ranks, I always felt a deeper sense of anxiety that something would have to give; the unyielding tension between my increasing demands and the shrinking resources I had available to meet them felt perilous.

Over time, it seemed like work was just one long and stressful pattern marked by: intense periods of activity (where it didn't seem possible to get it all done), punctuated by moments of relief (when things miraculously came together in the eleventh hour), before a new period of intensity accelerated again. Although things always seemed to work out, the strain from these cycles left me feeling exhausted, and I began to wonder about the true costs of this unsustainable routine. Then, I found out.

One particular day, mired in a period of stressful intensity, I frantically drove to a client meeting. I was already late because it was the second "Wednesday at 10:00 am" meeting of the day. I was double booked again, which was an indicator of how I pushed the limits of what was possible in my effort to be everywhere and to say yes to everything. Pulling into the parking lot, I realized my heart was pounding and I was having trouble getting a full breath. Alarmed, I told my colleague what was happening, and she said it sounded like I was having a panic attack.

I denied it immediately, arguing that I did not feel panicked at all. Driving a bit fast probably elevated my heart rate, but I knew I did not face any mortal danger or overtly intense warning that could trigger that kind of physiological reaction. Despite my denial, my colleague turned to me and simply said: "You and I might know that, but your nervous system thinks it is under serious threat. You have to slow down!"

It turned out that I was having a panic attack. After a few more such episodes and an eventual doctor's appointment—voilà—I had my wakeup call. It was there the whole time, but I was too busy to notice and too wrapped up in my work to recognize just how affected I was. I didn't understand it at the time, but I was stuck in the manager's dilemma. At that moment, I faced one its biggest deceptions: *the belief that I couldn't stop even though I knew I couldn't keep going.*

With strict advice to reduce my stress levels, I began to reevaluate how I worked. I knew I wanted to make some changes, but the question was how? To begin, I started with my overflowing plate of responsibilities that never seemed to diminish, no matter how many to-dos I checked off the list. I quickly realized that I had very little control over the load that I carried. The economy and the organizational dynamics that enabled the "do more with less" attitude was not going to change anytime soon, no matter how much I personally needed to simplify things.

Accepting this inevitability left me with the other side of the equation to work with, and so I began to focus on *how I responded* to the load. Specifically, I considered what I did (or did not do) that made things more hectic and complicated and what specific triggers seemed to lead me back into that overwhelmed cycle. As I began to see my situation for what it was, I made two important discoveries. First, I realized that I had much more influence over my total experience than I previously believed. From the day-to-day choices I made, to the specific ways in which I approached my responsibilities, I could not only improve the quality of my experience during the spikes of intensity, but I could actually do certain things to get ahead rather than just tread water.

The second discovery was that I was not alone. I recognized a similar dynamic among most other managers. Despite the fact that each person's circumstances showed up differently, the same cycle of near-continuous stress and periodic calm was a persistent and troublesome theme in our working lives. Moreover, as the frequency and impact of our overflowing workloads only increased, the effects from these cycles posed a growing concern at all levels of leadership.

As my career evolved and I shifted from leading teams and organizations to externally coaching and consulting with organizations and their diverse leaders, I made a third discovery that formed the seed crystal of this book. I realized that a similar version of this experience was shared in some form by nearly every manager I encountered. It reflected a fundamental challenge that connected us across industries and sectors, as well as boundaries of age, rank, gender, and geography. Looking back, these three insights were the catalyst for *The Manager's Dilemma*.

Drawing on the lessons I've learned as a manager and consultant to countless others, I wrote this book to be an *experience guide* for anyone feeling undermined by the impossible expectation of producing more and better work with less time and fewer resources to get it all done. Whether you feel the slow burn or acute pain of this inverse equation, I hope these insights and tools provoke a healthy confrontation with yourself because you don't need to wait for a panic attack or some other wakeup call to come to terms with what isn't working in your life at work.

While your success as a manager might be determined by the outcomes and results you deliver, your success as a person is determined by the quality of the experience you have on your way to figuring it out. If you manage people, priorities, and projects, this book can help you find your way.

JESSE SOSTRIN,
October 2014

ACKNOWLEDGMENTS

I WOULD LIKE TO THANK MY EDITOR, Laurie Harting, for a great collaboration and for continuing to trust in me to deliver. I would also like to thank my editorial assistants, Bradley Showalter and Alexis Nelson, for the behind-the-scenes support that made the process of getting this book out to the world seamless.

PART 1

EMBRACE THE DILEMMA

Successful managers solve problems, but problems are like holes in the ground. Our solutions fill them with dirt, but that only gets us back to level ground.[1] As more problems show up, we repeat the exhausting process until the cycle drains our capacity and eventually buries us. If you want to do more than exchange recurring problems for temporary solutions, know that *some challenges cannot be solved*. Managers face an intractable situation where there is not enough time, energy, resources, or focus to meet the increasing demands they face. This impossible circumstance is a true dilemma, but there is a better response than just shovels and dirt. To gain this leverage, you have to understand the origins of the manager's dilemma and come face-to-face with the causes and conditions of your own.

INTRODUCTIONS

THE MANAGER'S DILEMMA EXPLORES THE widening gap between the increasing demands we face and the shrinking resources we have available to meet them. However, this is not a time management book to deal with the avalanche of e-mails, meetings, and tasks dropped on your plate. Nor does it offer a packaged set of clever work-arounds to deal with the overflowing and stressful priorities you face. As you will see, it is time for managers to take off their capes once and for all; the superhuman notion of getting more and better work done with fewer resources is a profoundly damaging myth whose time has passed.

Instead, this is a book about the effect that *living within the gap* has on one of the largest categories of workers in the world: the millions of managerial professionals embedded within every sector and industry of our economy. More importantly, it is a book that reveals how the tension between shrinking capacity and increasing demands forces us into an unwanted status quo where we constantly struggle to make progress, but never really catch up.

Regardless of your experience and rank, if you are responsible for managing people, projects, and priorities, then you are susceptible to this vicious experience that I call *the manager's dilemma*. When it emerges for you, it not only reduces your productivity and effectiveness in the short term, but also erodes the quality of your working life in the long run.

Considering the scope and importance of the topic, I wanted to start the book with a remarkable introduction. When I thought about the perfect way to introduce it, I considered setting the tone with a series of *thought-provoking questions* that would leave no doubt about the importance of the book's evocative concepts:

- Why are managers flooded with practical advice and credible solutions about what they should do—yet those prescriptions so often fail to make an impact?
- Why do so many managers work hard, follow their plan, and do everything right—yet still fall short of the outcomes and experiences they want?
- Why—despite herculean efforts—is there never enough time, energy, resources, or focus to meet the demands managers face?

At first, I believed that questions like these could stir both curiosity and a deeper sense of urgency to understand what the dilemma is and what can be done about it. But in the end, I realized that these and other important questions need more room for adequate exploration, so I decided they would have to wait to be fully unpacked throughout the chapters.

Abandoning the questions, I wondered if a better introduction would be a series of *compelling statistics* that would hit the reader hard with unavoidable facts, like a gut punch right out of the gate. For example:

- a full 58 percent of managers say they did not receive any management training[2];
- 80 percent of managers say that the demands they face are increasing[3];
- 66 percent say "workload" is the top cause of their stress, outranking "people issues" and "job security"[4];
- nearly half of managers say they struggle with a lack of focus and clear direction[5];
- 61 percent of managers say they are working below their optimal level of energy[6];
- 51 percent say increased workload has a direct, negative effect on their well-being[7]; and

- over 25 percent of managers admit they were not ready to lead when they were promoted.[8]

While I find numbers like these compelling evidence for the ubiquitous presence of the manager's dilemma, I wanted a single data point that could somehow tell the story of the book in one powerful statistic. Then I found it—a simple but undeniable measure from a Corporate Executive Board study that revealed: *The average manager has 12 direct reports, compared with 7 before the recession.*[9]

At face value, this leap represents a 40 percent increase in the average manager's workload. Between the lines, this means a significant draw on the dwindling time and resources associated with everything managers do, from setting expectations, to establishing priorities, monitoring accountabilities, supporting ongoing productivity, and managing the countless small moves required to sustain the overall effectiveness of their teams. Said another way, it is 40 percent more goal-setting discussions, weekly check-ins, difficult conversations, annual reviews, and so on.[10]

Initially, I was convinced that this would be an exceptional introduction to the book. Both as a statistical fact and as a powerful metaphor, there is a 40 percent drain on your already limited capacity to do what you need to do in the way you want to get it done. This stark number forces you to confront an inevitable question: *Where does your additional 40 percent of time, energy, resources, and focus come from to meet the demand?*

Compelling statistics, a better way to open the book? *Statistically, you're likely to derail because companies fail to hire the right candidate for managerial positions 82 percent of the time.*[11]

Despite the logic of the numbers, I still did not feel like this was the best way to start *The Manager's Dilemma*. After all, it is a book about the real experience of managers and not about statistics—no matter how compelling. So I wanted to brainstorm a story, *a metaphor*, or a clever anecdote that could take readers beyond the numbers in order to paint a fuller picture of this complicated phenomenon.

Then, I struck gold: *"An umbrella at home won't keep you dry in the rain."* This obvious, but all-too-familiar, experience really does sum up an essential aspect of the book. The truth is that managers know what they need to do, and in most cases they even know how to do it. However, because of the dilemma's distracting effect, all of the best practices, first-class advice, and logical prescriptions intended to ease our stress and resolve our challenges are just an umbrella sitting by our front door when we've already rushed out of the house and into the storm.

There are thousands of management books about selecting the right umbrella and avoiding storms, but this is a book about *how you ended up without yours at the precise moment you needed it most*. Even more to the point, it is a book about the practical changes you can make to eliminate those hectic days that cause you to rush out and forget it in the first place.

I was certain that this was precisely the kind of pithy introduction that would intrigue readers, but I ultimately decided against this one too. No matter how creatively it might set the tone, *The Manager's Dilemma* is not a high-concept argument; it tackles concrete challenges and presents time-tested tools to resolve them. Therefore, I knew that the introduction needed to be more direct than some abstract analogy. To achieve this (and because the manuscript was due), I chose to go back to basics with a simple statement for the opening line of this book: *There is not—and never will be—enough time, energy, resources, or focus to meet the demand.*

This is not hyperbole or negative thinking; it is a by-product of structural forces in the economy and society that have combined to squeeze more out of worker productivity while providing fewer resources to sustain those gains. Unfortunately, this is not a new phenomenon either.

For generations, credible voices have described the dangers of what we have literally baked into the role of managers.[12] From epidemics of managerial burnout, to the current tidal wave of disengagement that affects leaders and their teams in profound ways, the signs have been there all along. This book just interprets the writing on the wall. Every manager, no matter how talented or experienced, is now vulnerable to the dilemma's push and pull because it is an intrinsic part of work.

PROBLEMS WITH NO SOLUTIONS

This is not a book about managing your time better, using your energy more wisely, or acquiring resources more ambitiously. Those things help, but in reality the book does not promise conventional solutions because by definition, a true dilemma is unsolvable. Dilemmas cause a tug-of-war between the two competing ends of the continuum where equal and opposing forces (both imperfect and therefore undesirable in some way) remain in tension. The manager's dilemma reflects this push and pull of irreconcilable choices that are at the heart of what makes leading so difficult.

- Which goal rises above all your other priorities?
- Which "fire of the day" gets extinguished while others are selectively ignored simply because there are too few resources available to put them all out?
- Which project receives funding while other high-potential opportunities languish?
- Which team member gets your attention as other deserving candidates are inadvertently overlooked?

These are just a few examples of the critical assessments, judgment calls, and decisions that frame the ultimate concern for managers. Within each of these difficult questions, you see the endless set of trade-offs managers must make when stuck in the dilemma. In this zero-sum game, each managerial move generates a give or take with vital consequences for the team and organization. More importantly, it leaves managers caught in a cycle where there is always unfinished business.

This treadmill effect is the dilemma's calling card. In an environment of competitive extremes, *how a manager approaches his or her dilemma becomes the crucial pathway to either breakthrough and success or burnout and failure.*

> Would you rather drink from a fire hose, or have your well run dry? "Neither" is just not a realistic option when you're stuck in the manager's dilemma.

THIS IS THE MANAGER'S DILEMMA

When something affects all of us in unique ways, it can be tempting to conclude that it just cannot be identified accurately. However, even with its diverse characteristics and highly subjective nature, the dilemma is crystal clear when you get up close:

> *It's the easy improvement you don't have time to make…*
> *It's the good advice you don't have the energy to follow…*
> *It's the logical next step you're too resource-strapped to take…*
> *It's the obvious solution you're too distracted to notice…*

When the perpetual gap between the increasing demands you face and the shrinking resources you have to meet them widens past the point of no return, the manager's dilemma takes hold. In an effort to catch up and stay afloat, you inadvertently begin to work against yourself in counterproductive ways that make your solutions powerless, your advantages weak, and your already scare supply of time, energy, resources, and focus even more tenuous.

The harder you struggle to meet the impossible demand, the more you lose the very performance edge that you need to break the cycle. Within the dilemma, shortcuts become dead ends, and the unending struggle to do more with less leaves you exhausted and unable to meet your full potential. When you can't work any harder, but doing less is equally unrealistic, you're stuck in the *manager's dilemma*.

GOING BEYOND THE DILEMMA

The goal of this book is to help you see your dilemma clearly and then apply practical tools to immediately start moving beyond its grasp. With this purpose in mind, I offer a collection of insights about the real working lives of managers. Some chapters are provocative expressions of the obstacles and trapdoors that threaten to derail us, while others are more like field guides with actionable recommendations to alleviate the immediate challenges that keep us stuck in the dilemma. There are no shortcuts or quick answers, but the straightforward insights and proven tools can easily be applied with your focused attention.

Because this is a book about the everyday challenges managers face, the cases and illustrative stories are based on real people and their very real experiences. Pulled from my coaching, consulting, and internal leadership experience, they are written to help you see what connects us through this widely shared experience. In some cases, names and details have been altered.

Part I tells the origin story of the manager's dilemma and then brings you face-to-face with your own. It helps you to reconcile the fact that the split between undesirable alternatives is not a problem to be resolved, but a structural inequity to acknowledge. As you "Embrace the Dilemma," you accept it for what it is, and that helps you see it clearly. With a new perspective, you gain leverage to respond better. Wholly embracing the dilemma produces what reputed Wharton professor Katherine Milkman calls the *fresh start effect*[13] where you can drop the baggage and wipe the slate clean of the habits and automatic responses that got you stuck in the first place.

Once you embrace the dilemma, you have the opportunity to "Balance the Equation." Part II identifies specific *stabilizers* that can stop your slide deeper into the dilemma by finding this balance in the chaos. This disrupts the dilemma's hold and positions you to use its greatest weapon against it.

If the dilemma's core logic is to colonize your working life with challenges that simultaneously disrupt your performance and drain your precious time, energy, resources, and focus, then you have to restore them in ways that not only rebuild your capacity, but also concurrently boost your learning and performance. This is how you convert a double negative into a dual positive and beat the dilemma at its own game.[14] As you apply proven techniques to balance the equation, you stop using compensatory energy to simply tread water by reacting to one problem after another, and instead increase your capacity to choose the meaningful direction you want to pursue.

Part III is about leveraging these *multipliers* to enhance your efforts and give you the escape velocity you need to move beyond the dilemma. The principles enable you to actually "Flip the Scales," so rather than continuously losing ground to the manager's dilemma, you will implement specific strategies and tools to gain ground and accelerate the impact you want to have on your team and on the organization.

The heart of the book includes a series of eight principles and practices that reveal the dilemma's core challenge and show you how to move beyond them. It turns out that the dilemma's triggers are swinging doors and within each one there is an alternative path that acts as an escape hatch. To exit the dilemma, you have to go out the way you came in:

1. The dilemma leaves us feeling trapped with unwanted options on all sides, so *follow the contradiction* to loosen the grip of the dilemma.
2. It turns us around and distorts our values and goals, so *determine your line of sight* to focus on the right priorities.
3. It spins our wheels, causing extra effort with less effectiveness, so *distinguish your contribution* to make a deeper impact.
4. It punctures leaks in our already fragile time, energy, resources, and focus, so *plug the leaks* to restore your capacity.
5. It forces us to accomplish unimportant stuff, so *create the conditions* you need to achieve more value.

6. It leaves us powerless and unable to impact our circumstances, so *find the pocket of influence* to use minimal effort for maximum impact.
7. It limits our ability to use everyday obstacles for good, so *convert your challenges to fuel* and turn the tables on the dilemma.
8. It threatens us, forcing a divisive "us vs. them" competition, so *make your goals their priorities* and strike the mutual agenda.

Together, these eight drivers and related responses can change the way you work. If the book was a seminar, our objectives would be to: (a) identify what fuels and sustains the manager's dilemma; (b) recognize the specific effects your dilemma has on you; (c) understand and apply eight proven strategies to overcome it; and (d) develop sustaining momentum to avoid lapsing back into it.

Beyond these goals, my hope is that the book helps you to be *happier and more successful* at work, however you define that. In your transitions, in your critical moments, and in your everyday experience of getting the job done, the inner game is yours to play. In order to ease the tension of a dilemma, you have to go to the heart of it and embrace what you find.

Chapter 1

THE EVOLUTION OF A DILEMMA

It begins when our overloaded working lives tilt us into the *Danger Zone* where counterproductive habits accelerate the dilemma's undermining effect

THIS IS A BOOK THAT COULD HAVE BEEN written 35 years ago with nearly the same urgency and poignancy. While the reference points may be different and the jargon dated, the tinderbox has been building for several generations. The modern-day origin story of the dilemma goes back as early as 1981 when the *Harvard Business Review* began publishing articles that dealt with the growing concerns of managers who were overwhelmed by the struggle to cope with increasing demands and rapidly changing conditions.[1] And although this building pressure finally exploded at the inflection point of the Great Recession, the manager's dilemma was already embedded in our way of working.

The circumstances required for the dilemma to thrive were present long before 2008. More than a quarter century of cutbacks, downsizing, and increased competition established the inverse equation of shrinking resources and increasing demands. Over time, this structural deficit has unfortunately become an acceptable dynamic for managers to deal with, despite the unavoidable challenges it brings. In short order, these big external trends came home to roost for managers in tangible ways.

Originally exempt from labels like "burnout," which were reserved for the rank and file, the increasing pressures and compounding changes were the fertile ground that enabled the dilemma to take root. In this overmatched and often overwhelmed place, a variety of factors began to affect managers at alarming rates. These included:

- *Overwhelming lack of control.* When you feel unable to influence decisions that affect your job—such as your schedule, assignments, workload, or the resources you need to do your work—your resilience fades.

- *Unclear or conflicting expectations.* If you're unclear about the degree of authority you have or what bosses, peers, and direct reports expect from you, you're likely to feel uneasy and on edge at work.

- *Mismatch in values.* When your values differ from the way your clients, bosses, colleagues, and direct reports conduct business, the mismatch causes inner conflict and the dissonance takes an emotional toll.

- *Extremes of activity.* When a job is extreme or chaotic, it requires constant energy to remain focused. Without the effective management of time, energy, resources, and focus, the "boom/bust" cycles lead to fatigue and burnout.

- *Dysfunctional workplace dynamics.* Whether you work with unstable clients, an office bully, undermining colleagues, or micromanaging bosses and coworkers, any type of distressing situation can contribute to unrelenting low-grade or acute stress.

- *Work-life one-sidedness.* If your work takes up so much of your time and effort that you don't have the energy to spend time on personal renewal or valued social activities, you hit your breaking point sooner and are less equipped to rebound from the imbalance.[2]

These factors, which many managers confront at a very personal level, directly contribute to physical, emotional, and mental exhaustion. When they are severe, they can shake our confidence to the core and provoke doubts about our abilities, competence, and value. Regardless of what triggers these factors and their varying degrees of severity, at the end of the day it is all just *weight*, and the manager's dilemma materializes when we carry too much.

THE *ZERO MARGIN EFFECT*

One of the first, and still the best, thinkers to describe how our professional lives are threatened by the nature of this *weight* was the educational psychologist Howard McClusky. On the way toward developing his groundbreaking *theory of margin*,[3] the well-regarded professor wondered why some adults were able to successfully start and complete new projects, goals, or initiatives while others seemed to become quickly overwhelmed and unable to continue.

His research eventually led to a simple formula that expresses a relationship between the "load" a person carries and their available "power" to carry it. Expressed as an equation, we could say: *Load − Power = Margin.*

Your margin is what's left over after you expend your existing power to address your load. When you have a surplus, you not only meet your current demands but you can use your additional margin to increase your load in the form of new goals and so on. When you operate from a negative margin, your existing load is already too much to carry, and any new or unexpected challenges are likely to fail due to a lack of available capacity to meet the spike in demand.

Common external load factors include both the general circumstances and specific challenges associated with family, career, social, and economic obligations. Internally, load factors may include goals, personal expectations, and related thinking and decision-making demands.

Conversely, each of us also has a set of power factors that act as our vital resources to carry the weight and meet the demands of our load obligations. These can include resources such as: physical strength, stamina, energy, and health; emotional intelligence; critical thinking; economic supports such as access to money, power, and influence; and our general capabilities in the form of knowledge, skills, and abilities.

What McClusky found—hidden right there in plain sight—was that he could tell which individuals would finish the class, attain the degree, or succeed in their new project by assessing their *margin of power*. The key to avoiding false starts and failures was to carefully assess your available margin and to take on new efforts only after you intentionally increased your power factors to create the necessary surplus.

Herein lies the critical issue for today's managers: *How many of us really have a choice with what we are asked to take on?* The loads we carry are full of stuff mandated to us and we do not have the luxury of carefully considering our available margin before taking on new responsibilities!

This mismatch is one of the best ways to understand exactly what the manager's dilemma is. When nine out of ten of the managers that I work with say they do not have enough time, energy, resources, and focus available—and that their loads continuously increase in the form of greater demands—you have what I call the *Zero Margin Effect*.

This effect triggers the impossible situation of the manager's dilemma and its cascade of unwanted trade-offs. In this space there is always an unmet priority and an unresolved issue. The odds of successfully meeting all of these demands are reduced to zero and the math does not lie. Figure 1.1 illustrates the point at which the *Zero Margin Effect* kicks in. It is the moment when the demands you face increase past the point where your available power and resources can match them.

If your margin is dangerously low, or worse, has already moved past zero, your susceptibility to the dilemma increases significantly. One of the most predictable aspects of work is that something unpredictable will invariably emerge. It is this unpredictability of events in your working life that continuously threatens your delicate balance. So if you're already maxed then you have no "extra" resources on standby for the

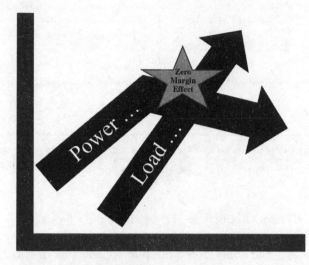

Figure 1.1 The *Zero Margin Effect*.

next unexpected emergency or assigned priority. When it arrives—and it most certainly will—it could be the challenge that tilts you precariously toward the *Danger Zone*.

TILT…DANGER…DILEMMA

In the simplest terms, we work on a spectrum of effectiveness. We are not always at our best, nor thankfully do we dwell at our worst. We typically slide along a continuum that varies with the ups and downs of work's natural rhythms. When we are in a good place, with available margin to deal with our load, we take a balanced approach to meeting our demands, use our strengths wisely, and sustain the capacity to manage well. Let's call this the *Performance Zone*, which is the place where we want to be.

As we confront our day-to-day demands from this place, we are more likely to be: response-driven, multidimensional, flexible, proactive, and engaged. However, when our margin runs low and the inverse equation of shrinking resources and increasing demands stresses our capacity to the breaking point, the strain can tilt us away from the *Performance Zone* and push us toward the *Danger Zone*.

Figure 1.2   The thin line between *Performance* and *Danger*.

Whether it is the stress over time that weakens us or the flashpoint of an unexpected demand that finally puts us over the top, once we slip into the *Danger Zone*, we are more likely to be: defensive, disorganized, delayed, disrupted, disoriented, and disengaged. Figure 1.2 illustrates the thin line between these two divergent zones.

Once we tip toward the *Danger Zone*, a switch gets flipped. Like a declining immune system worn thin by too many threats against it, the dilemma and its negative effects take hold. The instinctive shift into survival mode ignites a vicious cycle where our advantages lack impact and our solutions lose their power.

What does the Danger Zone *sound like?* The increasingly high levels of turbulence that push us toward the *Danger Zone* are so pervasive that evidence of them can be found in everyday language used to describe work. In a study at George Washington University,[4] students interviewed a wide range of professionals and generated a large number of familiar phrases, including: "getting hit by friendly fire," "dodging bullets," "the train leaving the tracks," and "being dead in the water." A person thriving in their *Performance Zone* would not use destructive words like these to describe their experience at work. These are the sounds of the *Danger Zone*.

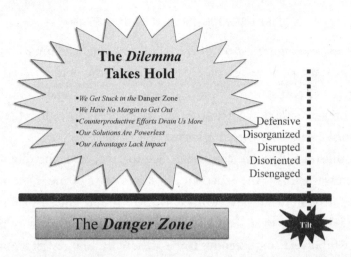

Figure 1.3 Inside the *Danger Zone.*

Desperation from the *Zero Margin Effect* can trigger counterproductive attitudes and behaviors that work against us, causing us to duplicate efforts and waste our remaining capacity. Even when we temporarily catch up, the ever-advancing demands outpace our renewal of resources and this ongoing deficit cycle sustains the dilemma. Figure 1.3 illustrates the way the manager's dilemma triggers a pattern that keeps us in the *Danger Zone.*

The manager's dilemma has characteristics of a living organism, and so I often personify it. Once you get used to seeing how it shows up for you, you may notice that it evolves with the rhythms of your work. When business is good, the dilemma spikes because the growth curve pushes everyone's capacity to the edge. When business is bad, the dilemma spikes because the belt tightening pushes everyone's capacity to the edge, just for the opposite reasons. Although the cycles of the dilemma come and go, it sustains itself by consuming your time, energy, resources, and focus.

To simplify these vital power factors, I will refer to them throughout the book simply as your *TERF* (*time, energy, resources, and focus*). In order to meet the demands you face and avoid the damaging effects of the manager's dilemma, *you have to protect your TERF.*

FIRST ENCOUNTERS WITH THE DILEMMA

The most damaging aspect of our slide into the dilemma is that we develop unproductive response patterns that stay with us even if and when our circumstances improve. These habits stay static until something breaks them down. However, it's in the breakdown that the reconciliation of what's not working becomes possible.

To illustrate how we can come face-to-face with our dilemma in sudden ways, this is the experience of Don Marrs.[5] I met Don in 2006, and I am grateful to have worked with him and gotten to know his remarkable story over the years. Don spent his first act working as a successful advertising executive at one of the world's largest and most well-respected agencies.

After a meteoric rise through the ranks, Don's working life became increasingly complicated by new opportunities and rising expectations from the company. Not only were these expectations difficult, but they were compounded by the personal challenges he faced during a long and difficult divorce. Believing he could just apply the same hard work and intuitive judgment that got him to this point, Don powered through the increasing demands as his margin declined rapidly. Later, Don would say, "I was frequently tired and had gained some weight, but for the most part, there were no signs that anyone else could see," and so his slow tilt toward the *Danger Zone* stayed hidden.

One busy week, Don left for a Monday meeting in New York, only to return to the office in Chicago on Tuesday to prep for a Wednesday client presentation in Minneapolis, as well as a Friday meeting in Cincinnati that same week. Burning the candle at both ends, this was the kind of hectic schedule that set the pace for his overflowing set of responsibilities. Looking back, Don described that Wednesday meeting as the defining event that "made all the difference in my life from then on."

The president of the company was there, along with the head of marketing and a number of other research and advertising executives. The account was in good shape at that point, with a very successful campaign under way that was selling lots of product. As the meeting began, Don quietly reviewed storyboards and mentally rehearsed his close. When it was his turn, he stood up and turned to the audience, and then felt the blood rush from his face. I'll let his words describe what happened next:

> I opened my mouth, but instead of my voice growing stronger, it started weak and stayed weak. What I was saying sounded foreign to me, and ideas that had been important earlier were now dimming as I spoke. My mouth dried up, my shirt flooded with sweat, and the light in the room darkened to gray impressions. I couldn't remember what I wanted to say, or even why I was there. My mind had wiped clean. Standing there with no words, I felt like a slow-motion train wreck.

This was the moment that Don came face-to-face with the fact that he had been running on empty and the manager's dilemma had taken root in his working life. What once came easy was now painfully difficult. What once energized him and ignited his passion felt exhausting and futile. Moreover, the skills and abilities that once contributed to his success were no more than a distraction from the truth that there was just not enough TERF to get it all done. The bottom line was that he wasn't the manager he wanted to be, but more importantly, he wasn't the person he wanted to be either.

Like so many managers, Don had been edging closer and closer to that place, but he did not realize it until he was waist-deep in the dilemma. In the weeks leading up to that disastrous meeting, there were subtle clues everywhere, but he overlooked them thinking he could rally by relying on the same quick thinking and nose-to-the-grindstone approach that worked in the past. However, with no available margin to manage his increasing demands, a crisis moment was inevitable.

Sometimes we get a subtle wake-up call, but other times we slam into a brick wall. Don's story is only extreme because the depths of his dilemma surfaced all at once in a public setting. For most of us, our dilemma shows up gradually in ways that only we can notice at first. Small warning signs might include zoning out repeatedly at important meetings, failing to remember key details (like what you promised your boss at the close of business the previous night), or the succession of nights and weekends you give up for work and the growing resentment you feel as it dawns on you that you're just paying too high a price for the working life you have.

Fortunately, Don had the courage to confront his reality and make a series of life-altering changes that had transformational results. If you are barely keeping your head above water—and feel like there is too much weight resting on your shoulders—then you may be close to the *Zero Margin Effect*. Do not wait for your crisis moment to make the positive shifts you need.

If you are already past the subtle warning signs, then knowing your dilemma is the first important step toward moving beyond it. Whether yours was precipitated by a series of major transitions that quickly wore out your capacity, or whether it was just the slow and steady accumulation of too many responsibilities, the point is that *you are where you're at right now.*

Chapter 2

KNOW YOUR DILEMMA

Because what you are unaware of controls you, and the dilemma has nearly imperceptible ways of constricting your performance and fulfillment on the job

ARE YOU STUCK IN THE MANAGER'S DILEMMA? If you manage people, priorities, and projects, then the chances are good that you have encountered the dilemma at some point or may even be struggling with its consequences right now.

If you are unsure, listen to the way you talk about your own work. The emergence of paradoxical statements like the following is the first sign that the manager's dilemma is settling into your atmosphere:

> *"I can't afford to relax because things are too busy right now."*
> *"I'm drained, but I have to set an example of perseverance for the team."*
> *"With so many deadlines and demands, some priorities will have to be sacrificed."*
> *"It's too crazy now; I'll focus better once things settle down."*

From the outside looking in you can see how backward statements like these actually are. If a friend said something like this to you, it would be easy to point out the flaw in their logic and show them how the undoubtedly counterproductive behaviors stemming from these attitudes will leave them more deeply entrenched in the dilemma. However, when it comes to our own situations, we're too close and too tangled to maintain this level of objectivity.

When we are stuck in our own dilemma, we somehow start believing that this is how work *has to be*. Over time, the effects from this way of thinking and working leave us feeling like there is truly no way out. What was easy is now difficult. What was enjoyable is now unsatisfying. What was just an inconvenient headache is now a crisis. What used to give us a sense of purpose now seems unimportant. This is the manager's dilemma, and when we are stuck within its grasp we struggle to act in ways that align our aspirations, values, and goals.

However, if we learn how to pay attention and read the signs of its approach, we can proactively sense our tilt toward the *Danger Zone*. For you it may be fatigue from the lack of rest during constant activity, or increasing irritability from waking up tired day after day. For others it could be the frustration from missed workouts, the bit of extra weight from poor diet, the disorientation from excessive travel, the feeling of isolation from that missed social time with family and friends, or the predictable sore throat that always comes after you've pushed past your limits for just a little too long. With a clearer understanding of your "signs," you can anticipate its emergence and come face-to-face with your dilemma

It's More Than Your Everyday Stress: There is a difference between episodic stress where you might say "I'm feeling maxed out!" and the consistent form of stress caused when you are stuck in the manager's dilemma. For one, stress increases when you have too much work, too little time, and too few resources to do it. A temporary imbalance of these factors triggers normal stress in the average person. If you are in an industry that has peak periods where your workload fluctuates significantly, then you may even be able to predict spikes in your level of stress.

The point is that these stressful periods are manageable, and they don't have to leave any residual effect. If you have healthy routines to cope with the normal pressures of work, then you can pass through typical stress periods and emerge more or less unscathed. In some cases, it may be this particular form of stress that keeps you engaged in what you are doing and gives you the energy to achieve more. However, when the stress goes from the good kind (i.e., a jolt of urgency to make it happen when the pressure is on) to the bad kind (i.e., compounding stress without a means to successfully cope with it), it can lead you deeper into the dilemma.

MEASURE THE DEPTH OF YOUR DILEMMA

Although there are many common features of the manager's dilemma, each of us experiences our own version. The frequency, duration, and impact can vary based on a diverse set of factors that influence our circumstances. The key is to know your rhythm and tendency. Whether you are just beginning to tilt toward the *Danger Zone* in the early stages of strain or nearing full-blown burnout from working within the manager's dilemma over a period of time, the better you recognize the character of your dilemma, the more you can maneuver through its impact.

To help you meaningfully determine the state of the dilemma, here are three increasingly advanced ways to measure the scope of your predicament. In many cases, "you just know it when you feel it," and if you've resonated with the words of this book so far, you may have already sensed the nature of your dilemma. To bring clarity and focus to your initial hunches, these three assessments will help you take your temperature in relation to the specific effects of the dilemma.

ASSESSMENT #1: YOUR INVERSE EQUATION

Consider each of the following questions and answer with either "Yes" or "No" depending on whether the statement is true for you:

1. Have the demands on you increased over the past several months?

2. Are they likely to stay elevated and/or continue rising?
3. If your demands have increased, have you gained enough additional TERF to adequately address them?

You are tilting toward the *Danger Zone* if you answered "Yes," "Yes," and "No" to these questions—a sequence that reflects the core dynamic of the inverse equation.

Just answering "Yes" to the first question alone places you at risk of moving closer to the *Zero Margin Effect,* which makes you increasingly susceptible to the manager's dilemma. If you experience pressure from the inverse equation for too long, then the gap between you and your ideal *Performance Zone* widens and some telltale signs begin to show up.

These gaps impact your natural productivity cycles by extending and intensifying the negative swings. For example, imagine you typically start your week focused, energetic, and excited, but as unexpected demands and stressors increase, you turn scattered, fatigued, and frustrated. As the dilemma sets in, you will spend more time feeling the fatigue and frustration, and it becomes increasingly difficult to regain your positive energy and focus. In good times, this natural productivity pattern has a predictable rhythm and flow and you're able to confidently rely on your strengths to make it through the brief period of adversity. But while in the dilemma, your strengths are limited, your confidence declines, and so the pattern deepens and stagnates around the negative experiences.

Once your equilibrium is disrupted and your patterns of productivity shift, then indicators like these will also accumulate at an accelerating pace: You start by feeling used up, spent, and unable to generate fresh ideas and energy. You then experience a continued loss of motivation and interest in your work. Next, the physical and/or mental fatigue turns into a deeper sense of exhaustion. Ultimately, this leaves you feeling like you're just "going through the motions," with little passion for the future.

ASSESSMENT #2: THE PRESENCE/ABSENCE TEST

If you are struggling with the inverse equation and its effects, you need to take the next assessment to determine how far you have gone. The following ten-question assessment will determine if you are past the tilt and now squarely entrenched in the *Danger Zone*. For each statement in table 2.1, answer "Yes" or "No" if you have experienced the feeling or behavior at least once in the past month.

If you answered "Yes" to at least *four* of these questions, you are in the dilemma's grasp. If you answered "Yes" to *five or more*, then you are entrenched in it.

Once characteristics like these become present in your experience, they are much more than just passive attitudes. They start to shape your choices and behaviors in profound ways, and your actions have

Table 2.1 Early indicators of the dilemma

1. Do you feel frustrated or cynical about work?	Yes/No
2. Has the pace, quality, or impact of your contribution declined?	Yes/No
3. Are you critical of your bosses, colleagues, or direct reports?	Yes/No
4. Are you physically and/or emotionally fatigued?	Yes/No
5. Is it a challenge for you to go to work and get moving once you arrive?	Yes/No
6. Do you quickly lose patience with customers or clients?	Yes/No
7. Do you hold back contributions because it's not worth the effort?	Yes/No
8. Do you lack the energy you need to remain consistently productive?	Yes/No
9. Are you unsatisfied with work, even when you accomplish things?	Yes/No
10. Do you feel uncertain or concerned about your future?	Yes/No

an impact not only on your own performance, but also on team and organizational performance in tangible ways. As these early indicators accumulate, you may be:

- less likely to innovate or seek creative solutions to problems;
- less likely to invest time developing others or to hold them accountable;
- more likely to fail to meet stretch goals, priorities, and deadlines;
- more likely to blame others for problems and to take a cynical approach to challenges;
- more likely to suffer the effects of chronic stress at work; and
- more likely to stay in the job, even after mentally "quitting."[1]

ASSESSMENT #3: MEASURE THE DEPTH OF YOUR DILEMMA

If the presence/absence test confirmed that you are in the dilemma's grasp, this final assessment will measure the depth of your dilemma. Notice the subtle overlap between each assessment, which is by design. The intent is to reveal your own subjective experience with the dilemma, one layer at a time.

This final tool in table 2.2 was inspired by the 1963 work of Howard McClusky[2] and the 1996 research of Peter Vaill.[3] I created an early version of this TERF self-assessment in 2003, which I initially used with individuals caught in unresolved conflict and then later with managers bogged down in unsuccessful change initiatives. Subsequently, I expanded it to assess the specific depth of the manager's dilemma.

To complete the self-assessment, pick a time horizon when you think your dilemma first showed up and stick with that reference point as you consider each statement (i.e., "the past 30 days," or "the past 90 days," etc.). After reading each statement, select a number that accurately reflects your experience in that period. For best results, rely on your gut-level reaction and do not overthink your rankings within the five-point scale.

Table 2.2 Measure the depth of your dilemma

Key:

−2: Much less often

−1: Somewhat less often

0: No change

1: Somewhat more often

2: Much more often

T (Time)

1. I feel rushed and unable to keep up with my work	−2 −1 0 1 2
2. I take short cuts in an effort to get more done	−2 −1 0 1 2
3. I do not have enough time to accomplish what I need to	−2 −1 0 1 2
4. I don't take breaks for fear of falling behind even more	−2 −1 0 1 2
5. I bring my work home and have a hard time turning things off	−2 −1 0 1 2

E (Energy)

6. I am tired and lose my concentration easily	−2 −1 0 1 2
7. I get drained by frequent, unexpected challenges	−2 −1 0 1 2
8. I react first, rather than reflecting on how I want to respond	−2 −1 0 1 2
9. I get frustrated dealing with difficult people and situations	−2 −1 0 1 2
10. I wake up tired and then work too hard to feel rested	−2 −1 0 1 2

R (Resources)

11. I do not have enough resources to get everything done	−2 −1 0 1 2
12. The competition for limited resources causes tension	−2 −1 0 1 2
13. There are too many issues and problems to manage	−2 −1 0 1 2
14. I do not have the support network I need to call upon	−2 −1 0 1 2
15. I do not ask for or receive help from others	−2 −1 0 1 2

continued

Table 2.2 Continued

F (Focus)	
16. I feel distracted and unclear about my priorities	−2 −1 0 1 2
17. I do not stick with priorities until they are completed	−2 −1 0 1 2
18. Goals and objectives are handed to me, but I do not own them	−2 −1 0 1 2
19. My stress has increased, and I feel spread too thin	−2 −1 0 1 2
20. I repeat my efforts because things are incomplete the first time	−2 −1 0 1 2
Total Score:	

Your score is the net of the negative and positive numbers that you marked. Once you determine your total number (minimum possible score is −40, maximum possible score is 40), find the explanation for your corresponding range as follows.

1. *A score of 25–40* marks a *crisis* from the negative effects of the manager's dilemma. Each statement you scored with a #1 or #2 reflects a singular challenge from the dilemma, but taken together they represent a collective emergency. Not only has your short-term performance suffered from these effects, but it is likely that you're so entrenched in the *Danger Zone* that you're at risk of derailing if things do not change.

2. *A score of 15–24* marks a *significant impact* from the negative effects of the manager's dilemma. Each statement you scored with a #1 or #2 marks a point of urgency, where the impact of the manager's dilemma has potential to undermine your ongoing performance and the quality of your work in severe ways. The failure to move beyond the dilemma quickly only increases your level of risk for deeper, career-damaging habits to form.

3. *A score of 5–14* is a *wake-up call*, signaling that the time is now to rebuild your eroding TERF and to transition back to the *Performance Zone*. Use each statement that you scored with a #1

or #2 as a firm reminder to stay alert, maintain and enhance your existing TERF, and guard your margin to ensure that you stay in front of unexpected challenges or increasing demands.

4. *A score of 4 or below* means you are in good shape and the limited weaknesses posed by your dilemma can be addressed with the preventative insights and tools in this book.

UNPRODUCTIVE RESPONSES TO THE DILEMMA

Now that you can visualize the character and depth of your dilemma, how will you respond to it? The rest of this book includes eight strategies to help you overcome the drivers that cause and sustain the dilemma, but in some cases you have to unlearn a few bad habits first. As I have coached managers on their journey through the dilemma, there have been a few typical response patterns—all unproductive in some way—that most people follow. Figure 2.1 depicts several of the most common reactions that I see.

Notice how this 4x4 diagram has two axis points, Growth versus Fixed Mindset[4] and Use versus Conserve TERF. The mindset axis refers to the individual's general sense of orientation and empowerment toward the dilemma's challenges, while the TERF axis refers to the level of risk they

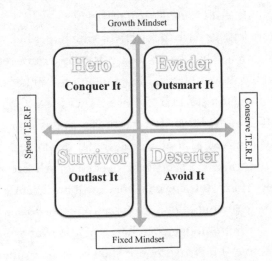

Figure 2.1 Four common responses to the manager's dilemma.

are willing to take in the use of their available resources. Depending on the circumstances, sometimes a person begins in one quadrant and then shifts toward another based on personal changes or the external factors of their situation.

In the top left, the *hero* wants to conquer the dilemma. They have a growth mindset, which means they believe that bad news isn't permanent and they can take ownership in the situation and make it better. The resilient hero is often a high performer, so he or she may initially think "the rules don't apply to me!" To match their "*bring it on*" attitude, the tools they use to try to get it all done come down to brute force. They use all of their available TERF freely in an effort to overcome the challenges they face and meet their rising demands, no matter how steep the climb may be. Once they deplete their margin and eventually begin to burn out, *heroes may become evaders.*

In the top right, we have the *evader* who simply wants to outsmart the dilemma. Believing that they can find a creative way to figure it out, they take a conservative approach to using their available TERF. They would rather avoid a confrontation with the brutal effects of the dilemma so they search for tools and tactics to sidestep what heroes encounter head-on. They also maintain a growth mindset, which enables them to confidently believe that they can stay one step ahead. When they finally exhaust all options, *evaders may become survivors.*

In the bottom left, we have the survivor who hopes he or she can just outlast the dilemma. They have "seen this before" and recognize that organizational life flows in cycles. They intend to hunker down as best they can until the latest storm blows over. They are willing to use their available TERF; however their fixed mindset causes doubt that any of their efforts will make much of a meaningful difference. As survivors hang back, they engage or disengage as needed for self-preservation and hope that their efforts to triage challenges will buy them enough time. When they finally run out of options, *survivors may become deserters.*

Finally, in the bottom right, we have the deserter who just wants to avoid the whole thing. In some instances, it is a quiet surrender, evidenced only by their steady lack of engagement and decline in per-formance. In other instances, they may vocalize the terms of the defeat and express their deep frustration and dissatisfaction about the circum-stances in an effort to take others with them.

While each of these four responses is understandable, they are also all damaging because they play right into the dilemma's core compe-tency. In different ways, the reactions not only leave us with the original lingering problems, but there is always ongoing baggage from the inef-fective response itself. In order to escape the dilemma's draining effects, you need a better response pattern—one that faces facts and goes all in.

For the heroes, take off the cape. For the evaders, know that you cannot run forever. For the survivors, surrender now and live to fight another day. Finally, for the deserters, you can be reempowered but there is a lot of work to be done. The first and best response to your manager's dilemma is to accept the situation for what it is and to focus all of your available TERF in a concentrated effort to balance the equation.

The goal of balancing the equation is to get to your break-even point, where the dilemma cannot take more than your available bandwidth. Part II introduces the next four chapters that enable this balance, which gets you out of the *Danger Zone* and back to level ground closer to your *Performance Zone*.

You won't find a reference to these pages in the table of contents. In the same way the manager's dilemma brings unexpected challenges to trip you up, here are a few hidden insights to help you go from embracing the dilemma *to* balancing the equation.

Managers are the lifeblood of organizations. They operate at the critical interface between the top leadership and the individual contributors that produce the day-to-day work that sustains the success of the company. Without the important connections they deliver, big picture goals and strategies would not relate to the everyday tasks and activities required to make them happen. Also, vital people, ideas, and resources could not align without this essential glue that managers deliver.

Despite the important role that managers play, there are some unflattering stereotypes out there that do not reflect this same level of importance. The manager's dilemma can take credit for one such analogy that paints a very different picture than "the glue that holds vital connections in place": *Rats in a maze, running an exhausting, futile, and unending race.*

The metaphor of the rat race has existed in popular language for 75 years, and although it applies to a wide range of circumstances it has special meaning for managers. If your interfaces between top leaders and employees feel more like closed doors and dead ends, then you may be confined to the maze. If the important connections you facilitate among people, ideas, and resources feel more like administrative hoops than innovative synergies, then you may be caught in the loop. If you no longer feel like the prized lifeblood of the organization, but instead just keep giving your blood, sweat, and tears without passion or reason, then you may inadvertently be running the race.

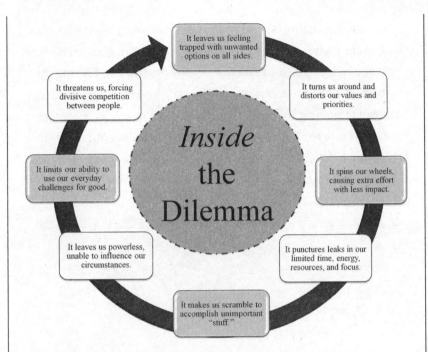

Figure 2.2   Inside the dilemma.

For managers stuck inside the dilemma, the race feels rigged. In Figure 2.2, each of the dilemma's negative effects acts as a barricade that keeps the loop intact. The eight compounding results "close" the off-ramps to keep you moving in the same endless beltway. Not only do these factors hurt our performance and the quality of our working lives, but they have the compounding effect of convincing us that we just can't stop even when we wise up to what's happening.

Sometimes you just know something and you don't need evidence or outside confirmation to believe it. If you feel like something is *off* about the toll your role as a manager is taking, then you face just such a choice: *Accept it and make a change* or *avoid it and just keep going in circles*. You know that you're too full of potential to stay on autopilot and look the other way, so there really is no choice at all. You have to make your move.

Despite the dilemma's apparently unassailable boundaries, subtle exits exist when you learn how to see them. The first move is to reject the race. This does not necessarily translate to leaving your position; it signifies a conscious reset of the rules that influence how you're willing to work. The final eight chapters represent a series of new expectations that can give you an avenue to choose something better. Following the principles and suggested practices will help you break the dilemma's hold and restore your performance capacity.

PART 2

BALANCE THE EQUATION

As you consider the origins of the manager's dilemma and come face-to-face with the causes and conditions of your own, you gain leverage to respond better. But just embracing the situation is not an indicator of success. If you want to stop wasting your time and energy working against yourself in counterproductive ways, then you need something more deliberate. To simultaneously weaken the dilemma's hold and restore your capacity to manage effectively, you have to *balance the equation*. This requires four strategic moves that limit the reach of the dilemma's destructive effects and lift you out from under the endless stream of demands to get you back to level ground.

Chapter 3

FOLLOW THE CONTRADICTION

Because the chink in any dilemma's armor is the subtle-but-powerful contradiction that loosens its absolute grip

THE MANAGER'S DILEMMA LEAVES US feeling trapped, with unwanted options on all sides. The trade-offs inevitably create an alignment problem that reduces our capacity to think and act in ways that are consistent with our values and priorities. This fracture is one of the dilemma's most perilous effects. Over time, the worn-out, off-course way of working ties us in knots and leaves us unsure about how to find our way back. Once inside the manager's dilemma, the fastest way out is to *follow the contradiction.*

Contradictions are the subtle clues that signal something is different than we thought it would be. These disruptions are important because our brains are wired to see what we expect to see, and we have the tendency to blow right past new information that challenges our old assumptions.[1]

Contradictions are literally the cracks in logic that allow us to both question our current attitudes and choices and see other

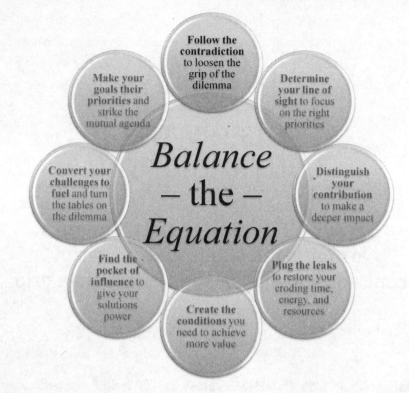

Figure 3.1 Follow the contradiction.

possibilities. A recurring thought, an uncomfortable feeling, an intuitive hunch—contradictions are everywhere and they can guide us through troubled situations. You follow the contradiction by noticing and learning from what is interesting, what stands out, and what doesn't quite fit.

I'm too busy to stop even though I know I can't keep going... this typical contradiction, which is a side-effect produced by the dilemma's constant pressure, makes it feel like there is no way out. But this is an illusion—one of the dilemma's best deceptions. There are escape hatches, but you have to know where to look. The chink in any dilemma's armor is the subtle-but-powerful contradiction that loosens its absolute grip.

The challenge is learning how to question the erroneous beliefs that we take for granted. For example, consider some of the Presence/Absence Test factors (table 2.1, chapter 2), and you can easily see the way contradictions become embedded into our way of thinking and behaving:

- I'm frustrated about work, but it's not worth the effort to figure out why.
- I am physically and emotionally fatigued, but I need to push through this busy period.
- I'm holding back my ideas because I'm frustrated that my boss doesn't listen.

Are these statements true? Of course the answer is "yes" if you believe that they are. But the bottom line is that there are other truthful possibilities as well, yet these are only accessible when you follow the contradiction.

When a person believes statements like these are true, then it is easy to visualize a whole system of attitudes and behaviors that work together—like armor—to hold these self-limiting beliefs in place. When they are taken for granted in the course of another frustrating, emotionally fatigued, withdrawn day, the contradiction protects its underlying assumption and becomes harder to penetrate the next time around.

Challenging our dangerous assumptions and other contradictions may lead us to see things we'd rather not see. However, if we ignore them or rationalize them away as little more than passing annoyances, then they cannot reveal the missing insight.

In this chapter, you will learn how to spot the contradictions within your dilemma so that you can follow the seam of daylight to loosen its hold and gradually move beyond it. To introduce the concept fully, I want to share my own story, which traces my discovery of the value of contradictions.

THE VALUE OF CONTRADICTIONS

It began during my first days on the job. I was immediately fascinated by the often unseen, but very powerful, patterns of interaction people engaged in day after day. After carefully watching the conversations between my bosses and peers, I got pretty good at noticing the subtle cues that signaled how things would tip in one direction or another. Over time, the physics of typical workplace interactions became some-what predictable to me:

> She gets angry and withdraws when he acts arrogant...That manager coasts, while his team members disengage, and they all pretend it isn't happening...Their weekly meeting will end in frustration again because they rush through another over-stuffed agenda that leaves important business unfinished, etc.

While I could not describe them with the same accuracy that I can now, I observed a wide range of these unproductive situations and my 21-year-old brain wondered simply: *why don't they just change things?* I did not know it at the time, but I had just discovered the most important question of my professional life.

Since those first naïve days on the job, I have led a determined pursuit of that question in its many forms: *If people know what the problem is, then what's the problem? Why is it so hard for people to change their attitudes and behavior? Why can't people see how they contribute to the very circumstances they say they do not like?*

I reasoned that some people really did want improvement, so there must be something keeping those old, unwanted dynamics in place, so *what is that thing?* After two decades of leading teams and organizations, as well as coaching other managers and leaders to do the same, I discovered that this "thing" is the *contradiction*.

It wasn't until I worked with a new manager named Jacob that I realized the core problem isn't just seeing contradictions; it is slowing down enough to pay attention to what they can teach us.

The Dilemma Up Close: It was Jacob's second consecutive staff meeting where people were much quieter than normal. The team's big project was moving into crunch time and Jacob had expected a lively discussion about the final punch list, maybe even a little debate about the best way to polish the deliverable. But things were decidedly flat, almost eerily quiet.

As he closed his computer and watched his team file out of the room, a question crossed his mind: *Is there something going on that I'm not hearing about... an issue that explains why people are so quiet?* He knew the team was worn out; the past two weeks had everyone staying late and coming in early. Moreover, it made sense that the lack of conversation could be easily explained by the exhaustion from those long days.

Snapping back out of this passing reflection, Jacob realized that he had to get moving quickly in order to make his next meeting on time. He didn't give it a second thought and the hectic day offered no room to revisit it any further...

CONTRADICTIONS ARE EVERYWHERE, IF WE SEE THEM

How can something either "be there" or "not be there" depending upon whether there is someone present to see it? It sounds strange but quantum physics has proved this concept. It is known as the "observer effect," and it proves that there can literally be something present if someone is there to see it. In the same way, contradictions are there if we see them (or not, if we don't). Because they are a key to going beyond the dilemma, this makes the discipline of learning to spot them an essential skill of managers. It actually isn't very hard because the dilemma itself is littered with contradictions, each one a clue to help us recognize the unsustainable and unproductive ways we work. Here are two more examples. Notice how the core contradiction produces a destructive pattern that only serves to reinforce the initial paradox:

- Rushing because you feel you can't slow down, producing work with errors, spending even more time fixing the mistakes that could have been avoided with more careful attention; and

- Knowing your plate is full, but still saying "yes" to new requests and piling more on, falling further behind, underdelivering, and feeling the pressure to say "yes" to more things to redeem yourself.

Contradictions and detrimental patterns like these surface everywhere in the dilemma. Outside of the dilemma, work is full of contradictions in general. One of the easiest ways to spot them is to look at the "breakdowns" we experience because they are *the lagging indicators of a contradiction*. As we manage complex people, projects, and priorities the gaps that make it hard for us to get our best work done often stem from what the internationally recognized sociologist Kingsley Davis called the "double reality."

In essence, there is always a double reality where, on the one hand, we have a complete system of attitudes and beliefs about "what ought to be," or what should happen in a given circumstance. On the other hand, there is the factual order of "what is." These two realities are not identical, but neither are they ever really separate.[2] The constant tension between our beliefs about how things should go and what people ought to do and say confound us time and again when they simply do not conform. To play with this idea, take a few minutes to review some of the relationship roadblocks you've encountered at work, and then create your own inventory of double-reality contradictions, such as: communicating a message clearly only to find out the other person heard something totally different, going above and beyond only to have your extra efforts unacknowledged, or giving someone the benefit of the doubt only to have the trust broken. There are visible contradictions leading up to breakdowns like these and they all hold a teachable moment if we follow them.

Beyond these interpersonal examples the very nature of our basic job descriptions also sustain a contradiction. For every one job description on the organization chart, there are actually two positions. First is the set of tasks and activities outlined in the standard role. The second is the set of hidden challenges each of us face as we confront the unexpected obstacles that come with managing change, collaborating with difficult people, navigating confusing workplace politics, and trying to get our best work done in an environment of shrinking resources and increasing demands. Nobody talks about it, but this double-reality affects us all. Over time, it creates what I call the hidden curriculum of work.[3]

A hidden curriculum exists anytime there are two simultaneous challenges where one is visible and understood and the other is concealed and undefined. For example, professional athletes master the fundamentals of their sport and excel at the highest level on the court or field of play, but they still have to learn how to deal with wealth, fame, and the many other challenges and distractions that come with professional sports. In the same way, the hidden curriculum of work[4] requires us to perform our jobs effectively, while we simultaneously try to figure out what the true demands are and how to get them done in a way that adds value to the team/organization and keeps our contribution relevant. There is perhaps no greater contradiction than the fact that what we are tasked with doing on paper does not always reflect the best use of our time, energy, resources, and focus for the organization or for ourselves.

From these wide-ranging, fundamental contradictions to the superficial inconsistencies that show up in our everyday interactions, they are everywhere once you start looking. In order to fine-tune our capacity to make the most of them, we have to learn how to see them in their many subtle forms.

LEARNING TO SEE

Contradictions can be a subtle voice in your ear saying, "This is interesting; maybe we should pause to see what's going on here?" However, the dilemma has a way of overpowering these important, but subtle, messages with justifications like: "Sure, that seems a little interesting…but you know we don't have time to sit around and contemplate, we have to get things done!" More times than not, the screaming voice carries the day and we move past the contradiction. In order to decrease the noise from the dilemma and amplify the subtle alarms of those meaningful contradictions, we have to have the courage to pause, see things differently, and wrestle with the paradox that can put you on the playing field of new insights.

The capacity to recognize and then follow the contradiction wherever it leads is one of the most important skills a manager can exercise. Unfortunately, the by-product of working faster, producing more, and always staying "plugged in" is a unique type of fatigue that causes attention compression. The truncated span leaves us unable (perhaps just unwilling) to recognize and consider complicated things that are nonetheless important to take into account. We don't slow down to look because we believe there is no time and it would be too inconvenient. Yet, the useful contradictions are there if we choose to see them. To regain your focus, you need curiosity, mental flexibility, and fearlessness.

CURIOSITY

As a coach and consultant, I have had the privilege of working with some amazing leaders, including prime ministers, governors, CEOs, university and foundation presidents, and heads of nonprofit organizations, who are changing the world. Over time I noticed that the smartest (and most successful) people I worked with had something in common. The unifying trait has nothing to do with how smart, tireless, and driven they are; it's an inner quality that is much subtler than these observable personality traits. When they encountered a new and unexpected situation, *they were curious and wanted to know what it was all about.* They did not rush to judge, name, or solve the problem, and they did not quickly reference their past experience to label this new thing as something "familiar." Instead, they were content to say "that's new and interesting" and to subsequently take the time to figure out exactly what *it* represents.

When every puzzle piece conveniently fits into the picture you already have in your mind, there are no contradictions, only biased confirmations.

These are not idle individuals with time to ponder the philosophi-
cal underpinnings of things; these are hard-charging, successful people
who could just as easily and convincingly classify the new experience
into their existing knowledge. But when people quickly say "I know
what that is!" they lack the curiosity and willingness to suspend their
judgment long enough to make room for something new. Here are three
prompts to help you develop your capacity to stay curious:

- *Ask what and why.* Explore the "what and why" about things
  without judging or concluding too much about whether they are
  good or *bad*. The spark of curiosity by nature is nonjudgmental.
  Following up with questions like "Why could it matter?" and
  "What effects does it produce?" is a healthy inquiry that reveals
  the contradiction.
- *Look for the underlying dynamic.* There is always more going on
  below the surface than we see. Focusing on the underlying root
  issues, values, meanings, and interests can widen our perspectives. If we take the presenting circumstances for granted, we
  often "look at the wrong problem" and miss the contradiction
  that lies beneath it.
- *Expect to see the unexpected.* When we challenge (and remind)
  ourselves to expect to see something new and different, we free
  our patterns of quick assumption making and put ourselves in
  a position to recognize and respond to what the contradiction
  presents. The danger of following assumptions, rather than contradictions, is that we can only see the same familiar picture.

MENTAL FLEXIBILITY

When I speak to audiences, there is inevitably one person in the crowd
who will ask the question: *What's the most important thing that managers
can do to succeed?* When I'm feeling cheeky, I say: *They can stop doing what
makes them fail!* Despite some claims to the contrary, there are no silver
bullets for guaranteed success. However, thanks to all of the type-A people
who want to cut to the chase, I have thoughtfully considered that question
regarding the fundamental driver of success, and I have an answer.

I believe the singularly defining contribution to the success of a manager is *how they respond to the unexpected*. Mental flexibility is the key to our response patterns because that is what enables our response competency to stretch during challenging, complex, and novel situations. Anytime the world suddenly looks and acts differently than it did the moment before, we rely on our mental flexibility to make sense of it and determine how we want to move forward. When faced with the manager's dilemma, the first thing to go is this fluid, flexible way of responding. In its place, a more rigid, self-preserving way of working takes over. Being stuck in the manager's dilemma is not a flexible place.

Two harmful impacts occur when we fail to follow the contradiction. The first is the lost opportunity cost of the missing insight that *could have been* revealed. It is impossible to measure this because it may have been nothing, or it could have been a paradigm-shifting insight that changed everything. The second and more palpable effect involves *insidious forms of courteous compliance*. This concept, coined by renowned psychologist David Kantor, feels exactly like it sounds: *You recognize that something is slightly off—a contradiction emerges—but due to a variety of factors (e.g., complacency, fear of speaking up, etc.), you stay silent and follow the flow. In essence, it's the subtle choice to be a bystander, not an active participant, and the moment of learning passes as the contradiction is forgotten.*

While there are many other factors that contribute to our overall success, how we *respond to the unexpected* is the trajectory-setting first step that defines what happens next. To increase our mental flexibility, we need to create more elasticity in our first response to the contradiction. This flexibility is produced through open-ended questions: What is truly new and different here? What is my first impulse about how to respond? If I follow that reaction, where will it likely lead? Is there a different response that could open up a new opportunity?

FEARLESSNESS

Along with curiosity and mental flexibility, we also need a degree of fearlessness to follow the contradiction. The safe little worlds we create in our minds not only feel good and protect us from painful thoughts that could challenge what we know, but they are biological and hard wired. In order to gain the benefit of a contradiction, we need to be willing to shatter those worlds even if the process can invoke fear, loss of control, and hesitation.

As they say over at NASA: "The coolest gases make the hottest rockets." How can you fearlessly embrace the contradictions in your working life?

For example, maybe you want to develop the courage to speak your mind more, especially when disagreement is likely. The contradiction surfaces when you simply go with the flow and set your own ideas and intentions aside. Whether out of fear of being wrong or being perceived as confrontational, you defer to others instead of acting. With a little more fearlessness, you could move beyond this compromise and know that *it's okay to be wrong* and that *guarding what you say* is the surest way to limit your impact.

Whether it is within the domain of personal and professional development or elsewhere, the presence of a contradiction escalates the tension we feel between what could be new, interesting, or important and the familiarity trap we get stuck in with our known, comfortable surroundings. Said another way, we have our own mental models where our tightly packed systems of belief and expectation provide us with a modicum of security in their predictability and a contradiction is a direct threat to that security.

One trick that works in the pursuit of this fearlessness is to use the language of "scenario testing." This relieves pressure that by seeing a contradiction *we must* confront and make difficult changes that will invariably be accompanied by some kind of personally challenging disruption. By giving yourself room for a reflective space where you can look at possibilities, compare/contrast scenarios, and contemplate alternatives, you focus less on the decisional aspect and more on the learning aspect. After stretching your thinking and taking stock of your capacity and readiness without the pressure to do it all right now, the right decision and best course of action is often clear and attainable.

LEARNING TO FOLLOW

The Dilemma Up Close: Remember Jacob, the manager who was introduced at the beginning of this chapter? After a series of crucial meetings, something was definitely off. It was crunch time for a critical project, and rather than lively discussion and engagement, his team was decidedly quiet and withdrawn. The contradiction was right there staring him in the face, but Jacob was too busy to notice.

It turned out that something was happening and the uncommon silence of his team was the *contradiction he needed to follow*. A disagreement among two associates had erupted and people began to take sides. Unfortunately, the chilly feelings showed up during the presentation to the client, and a choppy pitch led to a failure to win the business.

If Jacob had paused to follow the contradiction with fearlessness and curiosity when it surfaced, he may have been able to make peace and regain the collaborative edge for a winning pitch.

If you have ever been through the painful experience of discovering that someone lied to you, hindsight has a way of showing you that the signs were there all along. But without suspecting a lie in the moment, why would you pause to interrogate those minor details that didn't sound quite right? The dilemma lies to us, and we have to follow the clues that don't quite add up. Despite our impulse to avoid them, learning how to cross-examine its contradictions is the way through to the other side.

> The real frustration comes when you look back and realize that the clues were there all along, but you just sped past them. The key to being a present, engaged leader is to become observational. Being observational makes you more likely to adapt your style to leverage the situation at hand and meet the diverse needs of your clients and teams. It also makes it less likely that you'll get blindsided by unforeseen circumstances or miss the subtle cues that can alert you to emerging challenges and opportunities.

As you begin to exercise curiosity, mental flexibility, and fearlessness you will see contradictions in your everyday circumstances. In order to follow a contradiction you have to pause and spend time reflecting on what it is. Time is relative here; it could be a minute or it could be something you quietly consider in the background for days. You have to break through one of the dilemma's faithful contradictions to find this patience: "things are too hectic to pause and reflect!" At the precise time we could benefit from careful reflection, we convince ourselves that we cannot afford to take the time and so we rush ahead and miss the moment.

Releasing yourself from this counterproductive thinking requires the discipline of slowing down just enough to consider whether the contradiction is worth following. Once you do this, you can take the next two steps to get a handle on exactly what it is. It requires you to *break the logical force* and *get third-party insights*.

BREAK THE LOGICAL FORCE

When we respond to challenging situations, it often feels like we are on autopilot. Rather than choosing how we want to respond, the reaction "leads us." What drives our reactions in these situations is a kind of *logical force*,[5] which is a subtle-but-powerful habit that holds cycles of reaction and behavior in place. When we just react and follow the well-worn grooves of the same response we had last time, it is virtually impossible to follow the contradiction.

The examples I shared about my early career when I learned the value of contradictions clearly reflect the logical force that shapes our recurring habits of interaction: She gets angry and withdraws when he acts arrogant... That manager coasts, while his team members disengage, and they all pretend it isn't happening... Their weekly meeting will end in frustration again because they rush through another overstuffed agenda that leaves important business unfinished.

When recurring experiences like these take shape, the strong reactions push us toward the perception of what we "ought" to do and all the "shoulds, musts, mays, and cannots" that go along with it. Once we are stuck in the dilemma, these beliefs about what we "should" do get stronger and take on an increasing sense of inevitability. Over time, whenever that familiar context presents itself, the same limited set of choices emerges and the behavior we choose naturally follows the same experience of the past. Rather than stopping to evaluate what we want out of a given situation, we effortlessly replay a similar pattern of words, nonverbal communication cues, and attitudes that embody this sense of what we ought to do.

To break the logical force, you need to pinpoint the moment right before you shift into autopilot to resume that old familiar (typically unhelpful) response pattern. More than just a moment of reflection, it's a moment of choice for a different alternative.

GET THIRD-PARTY INSIGHTS

When you escape the inertia of these logical forces and begin to follow the contradiction, you may feel more confused and turned around in the short term. In these situations, it can be good to get third-party perspectives that allow you to contrast ideas and go beyond your own limited thinking. This is the equivalent of getting the devil's advocate point of view in order to affirm or revise your own sense of what you see.

To do this, simply identify someone in your support network and ask for a few minutes of their time: "I want to run an interesting situation by you when you have a few minutes. It could be nothing, but I think it is worth talking about out loud with someone like you." We all need these kinds of intelligent sounding boards to air out and unload what's on our minds, then to listen to how it sounds coming back to us in another person's voice. It is best to ask for others' time and insight when you're truly willing to follow the contradiction where it leads.

CHAPTER SUMMARY

THE EFFECT

The manager's dilemma leaves us feeling trapped, with unwanted options on all sides. This kind of suffocation creates an alignment problem that reduces our capacity to think and act in ways that are consistent with our values and priorities. Once inside the manager's dilemma, the fastest way out is to follow the contradiction.

THE HIDDEN INSIGHT

A resounding echo, recurring thought, uncomfortable feeling, or an intuitive hunch—contradictions are everywhere, and they can guide us through troubled situations. However, if we do not step toward them, they cannot reveal the missing insight. You follow the contradiction by noticing what is interesting, what stands out, and what doesn't quite fit.

THE RESPONSE

To follow any contradiction, you have to pause and spend time reflecting on what it is. It could be a brief moment, or it could be something you consider in the background of your mind for days. Once you pause and reflect, you must break the logical force that causes knee-jerk reactions and get third-party insights when you feel turned around.

THE SHIFT

Learning to spot contradictions and following them wherever they lead offers the seam of daylight you need to see through the dilemma. Rather than annoying inconveniences, contradictions become subtle truth tellers that we welcome because they can help us sidestep trouble ahead. Once you begin to follow a contradiction, you can move beyond some of the most damaging constraints of the dilemma by *determining your line of sight.*

Chapter 4

DETERMINE YOUR LINE OF SIGHT

Because the dilemma's noise and clutter will keep you chasing your tail and following shiny objects while your true priorities remain elusive

THE DILEMMA TURNS US AROUND and distorts our priorities. As a result, we end up pursuing goals and outcomes that are not necessarily important, valuable, or consistent with what we care about. Accelerating this "creep and drift" is one of the dilemma's specialties.

In order to rise above the clutter and the noise of the dilemma, you have to *determine your line of sight*. This critical connection can tether you to your priorities and provide direction when distractions multiply and the path forward is unclear.

The concept of a *line of sight* comes from compensation and goal theory, and it suggests that individuals perform better when they understand: (1) how their direct efforts impact their rewards and compensation; and (2) how their specific role uniquely contributes to the larger team and organizational objectives. In other words, we are more effective when we know what is important, how it affects us, and where our efforts fit into the bigger picture.

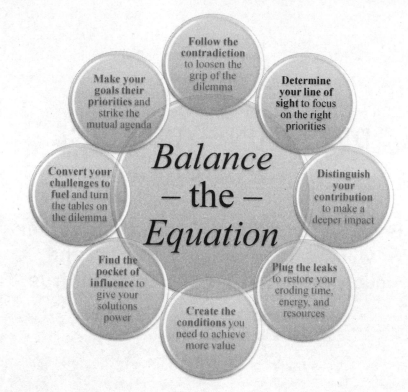

Figure 4.1   Determine your line of sight.

Your line of sight acts like a chain that positively hooks you together with the influencing factors, personal values, choices and commitments, and individual, team, and organizational goals that need to collectively influence your course of action. Even when you temporarily lose sight of these elements, the tether keeps you in the vicinity and helps to quickly close the gap.

When we operate without a clear line of sight, we lack the perspective to recognize what remains important as conditions shift. The net effect is twofold. First, we conduct a kind of whitewashing[1] that makes all objectives look the same. When we treat vital outcomes the same, we unconsciously divert our energy and attention away from our most critical priorities. Not only do the key goals remain unmet, but our already scarce TERF is spread thinner and rendered less effective as it is diffused.

The second prevailing effect from the clutter and noise of the dilemma is our tendency to practice skilled incompetence.[2] This causes us to unconsciously focus on the tasks and responsibilities that are easier and more satisfying to us, even at the expense of the more important, albeit difficult, priorities. When this "off-course" way of working becomes a habit over time, it erodes our capacity to perform at the level we want and sinks us deeper into the manager's dilemma. However, when we can discover a clear line of sight, we establish a solid connection to a clear way out of the chaos.

> It's one thing to be off target, but it is another thing altogether to be target-less, fundamentally unsure about what matters and how to pursue it.

Your line of sight is like a brilliant blue current cutting a distinctive wake within work's ocean of inconsistency. While others may not even notice it, it enables you to move with purpose, direction, and strength as the winds shift and competing goals and priorities knock you off course. When adequately clarified, a line of sight does several critical things simultaneously:

- it gives us stability, anchoring us at the intersection of multiple, motivating factors;
- it makes us selective when new priorities and challenges cloud our focus; and
- it gives us the rationale to say "no" intelligently as we say "yes" to what matters.

The strength of your line of sight correlates with your capacity to respond to the unexpected challenges and changes that make leading so difficult. The hard reality here is that everything changes and managing well is about maintaining the best combination of both "stay-the-course" commitment and "intentional flexibility" to adjust as changes happen.

As new information naturally recalibrates us toward new directions, do we automatically abandon the old? Understanding when to stay the course and when to intelligently evolve with change is an intuitive skill, and your line of sight is the guide.

At the heart of this concept is a straightforward question: *Where should I invest my time, energy, resources, and focus?* However, the question only looks simple from the outside.

The reality is that if we always had the right answer, we would never experience false starts, wasted efforts, or dead-end outcomes in our work. We would know our goals and anticipate our circumstances so well that the strategic and tactical path to success would be self-evident, we would create and deliver value through the effective management of our people, projects, and priorities, and a book like this one would be irrelevant.

But our goals can be elusive, our priorities can conflict, and our value to the team and organization is threatened as the world constantly changes around us. Therefore, it is this precise question that serves as the starting place to determine your line.

When it comes to "how" to craft yours, it needs to: reconcile your best opportunities with your realistic challenges; align your diverse priorities in a cohesive direction; and do both of these things without creating conflicting efforts that unnecessarily drain your TERF.

When it comes to the scope, it has to blend large and small vantage points. If you focus too much on the immediate tasks at hand, then you lose the energy and orientation that a "big picture" provides. If you consider just the big goals, then those can separate you from the emerging factors that require you to adjust on a choice-by-choice basis. Therefore, the scope of your line needs to mix the "big and small" so that you can be agile and committed simultaneously.

When well crafted, your line of sight serves as a point of multiple connections. It reveals how the things you do lead to what you want (i.e., efforts are connected to desired experiences, outcomes, and rewards). Going beyond the personal value, when you make it visible and worth discussing, it becomes a management tool for you as well (i.e., a reference point at meeting agendas, for delegation decisions, role clarification and alignment, etc.).

THE VALUE OF YOUR LINE OF SIGHT

A line of sight fills the space between the smallest and largest questions you wrestle with: *"What do I need to get done today?"* and *"Where do I want to go with my career?"* To pivot between the two it must be understood well enough to motivate you, but it does not have to always be perfectly clear. It is a work in progress that can advance with you as your career progresses.

Once established, it has a stabilizing effect on how you approach your responsibilities. From the very immediate focus on today's tasks to the longer-term perspective across the months and quarters, it provides the touch points to keep your vital efforts aligned.

One of the recurring questions I get when I speak to groups of managers is "What great leadership book do you keep on your bedside table?" Without hesitation, I say, "It's not a book at all; it's the note I wrote in response to the question: *What do I want from my working life?*" I follow up by telling the audience that their own go-to leadership library should contain the same thing. Without that clear definition of success, they may end up chasing others people's definition of success, which might look good, but satisfies no deeper meaning or value.

In the same way, you can think of a *line of sight* as this kind of penetrating insight—a focal point and fundamental understanding that organizes all other questions and decisions around a common purpose. To illustrate this concept, figure 4.2 depicts a line of sight that helped Ellen, a new manager, to make pivotal and time-sensitive decisions amid her conflicting priorities. In the image, each oval touches the line of sight and therefore provides a metric for evaluating choices and opportunities in a way that tests for alignment and maximum impact in multiple priority areas.

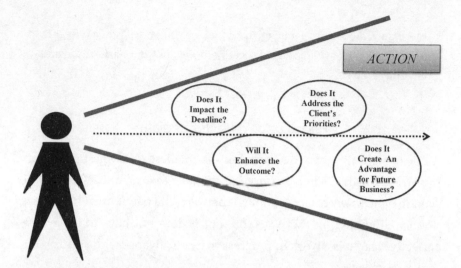

Figure 4.2   Line of sight for action.

The Dilemma Up Close: It had only been five months since Ellen's promotion to manager, but she already felt like a grizzled veteran. In that time, three of her six team members turned over, and the timeline for completing her major project was moved up by 30 days. Conditions were ripe for the manager's dilemma, and Ellen was tilting closer and closer to the *Danger Zone*. Before the promotion, she could keep her head down and just concentrate on getting her own work done. Now, she juggled the new layer of management responsibilities: delegating work and ensuring the performance of others while still getting her own assignments done concurrently. While the demands increased, her capacity to address them remained static.

The biggest challenge she faced was that she could not decide—among all of her existing priorities—what to focus on first to keep things moving. She needed to assess the experience of her new team members in order to assign them work; she had an intern that was a question mark as far as reliability was concerned; and she had increasing pressure from her boss about the technical requirements of meeting the updated timeline for the project's completion. The problem wasn't a lack of advice; in fact, it was the opposite. Team members helpfully offered input, and her boss offered more than his share of prescriptions, but as the quarterback of the team, Ellen needed her own *line of sight* to sort through conflicting suggestions and critical priorities.

To establish a line of sight for the project Ellen considered several key questions that enabled her to evaluate the merits of suggested technical adjustments offered by team members and other stakeholders. Once she identified these filter questions, she gained an immediate boost in confidence and was able to articulately (not frenetically) push back against the suggestions of others that lost a touch point to the line. It not only helped her manage the project to completion, but it became a communication tool that helped her team work better together.

Figure 4.3 also depicts a visual line of sight; however, this one is goal-driven and focused on long-term career advancement. It contrasts nicely with Ellen's example and shows the range of application for a line of sight. This one was created by an experienced manager who was ready

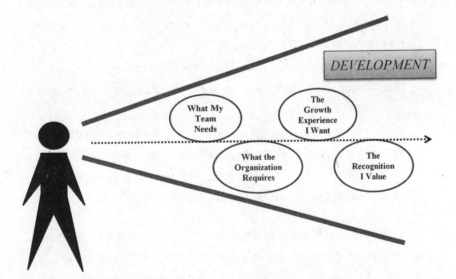

Figure 4.3   Line of sight for development.

to rebrand himself and chart an aggressive path toward the new opportunities he wanted to create. He was mindful of the fact that any choices he made had to allow him to continue meeting both his team's needs and the organization's priorities. However, he was firmly committed to finding new growth experiences and gaining critical recognition that would allow him to develop into a sought-after leader.

DETERMINE YOUR LINE OF SIGHT

Eventually you may want to maintain multiple lines of sight—one that charts your career trajectory, one that establishes your objectives for the year, and one that provides day-to-day direction on your immediate priorities can all fit nicely together. To gain confidence in the process required to determine your line of sight, begin with one and sketch it out by answering each question within this progression:

1. *What aspect of my work requires a greater level of alignment?* Get yourself in the right ballpark and determine an area that could benefit from a clear line of sight.
2. *Within this area, what are all of the factors that matter to me and to others that I have to satisfy?* Look widely at the possible elements essential to this line of sight.
3. *Which of these specific factors are important enough to track in my line of sight?* Now that you have the candidates, test the value and relevance of each one.
4. *If any one of these ovals fell away, what impact would that have on the outcomes and goals that this line of sight aligns?* Draw the line of sight with only the essential ovals intersecting the line. As a final measure, test each one to confirm its place.

This exercise is a starting place to help you craft a clear line of sight. When in doubt, remember that a line is more than just a set of goals. To understand the difference, consider the famous quote from Antoine de Saint-Exupery: "If you want to build a ship, don't drum up people to collect wood and don't assign them tasks and work, but rather teach them to long for the endless immensity of the sea."[3]

In this analogy, goals are *boats*, while a line of sight is the *longing for the sea*. Obviously boats matter, because after all, what good is longing for the sea if you cannot get out there to explore? The thing is that boats are easy once you have the purpose, drive, and conviction to build them. Your line of sight includes goals, but it touches the other motivating components that constrain or enable your pursuit of the goals.

FOUR OBSTACLES TO DISCOVERING YOUR LINE OF SIGHT

We all know that we are supposed to set a vision and maintain goals that can guide us through the everyday distraction and adversity we encounter. But why are so many of us unable to articulate the clear and compelling priorities that matter in our working lives? You can test yourself by trying to answer the following three questions in the next 60 seconds:

1. In your working life, what are your two most important priorities?
2. At work, what are the two most critical objectives you contribute to?
3. In your career, what are two of the most significant goals you must achieve to stay relevant and sustain the quality of working life you want?

If you are like most people, then your responses to these three questions came slowly and were likely incomplete. Even as you read these words now, you may still second-guess yourself, wondering why you couldn't do better. However, if the questions were different—Who are the two celebrities that have had the most embarrassing gaffes this year...Recite the advertising slogans of the two retail brands that you like most...List two teams that have the best shot at winning the championship next year—your page would more likely be full.

Are these questions more important than the first three? Why are we capable of listing facts, reciting miscellaneous information, and sharing personal opinions about trivial matters when more significant questions confound us? The reality for most of us is that we do not function with clear and personally relevant priorities that guide our attitudes, behaviors, and choices because what matters remains elusive, buried in the dilemma's distractions.

Whether you want to achieve something big, or just make a small change in your life or work, the path to any new experience or outcome begins when you know what you want. This focus is the motivating factor to create your line of sight in the first place. Once you zero in on that desire, establishing a clear and compelling line illuminates the path forward. To go from stuck in the manager's dilemma back to your *Performance Zone*, you have to overcome the four fundamental gaps.

WE MAKE PEOPLE GUESS

The first gap is that in the absence of clearly stating what matters, you will make people guess and they will likely guess incorrectly. Most frustration and conflict occur due to unmet needs. The irony of unmet needs and expectations is that they are often left unspoken. So when we rationalize ourselves away from clearly stating what we want, or what is most important to us in a specific situation or relationship, we may think that we are avoiding some confrontational pitfall. The fact is we are simply digging the hole deeper by forcing other people to guess our relative perspective and priorities and to take action accordingly. This is the reason why dashed hopes, passive-aggressive standoffs, and unresolved conflict in the workplace are such significant, repetitive problems. We are all pretty bad guessers when it comes down to it.

WE WAIT FOR PROGRESS TO COME TO US

The second gap is that getting what you want requires active movement toward it. It is self-deception to want something and remain standing still. Gaining the confidence to talk out loud about what matters is the first (and most important) active move. Once the picture of that desired future comes into focus and those around you are tuned in, you have to fight the attractive but unrealistic belief that the world will come to you.

An aspirational achievement requires you to step toward it, no matter how small those first steps feel.

WE BORROW OTHER PEOPLE'S DEFINITIONS OF SUCCESS

The third gap is that we are often very good at wanting what others want, but unpracticed at wanting stuff that is consistent with who we are and what we value. In his 2009 TED talk, Alain de Botton, the acclaimed writer, philosopher, and commentator on work, described the challenge of distinguishing what matters to us and the noise we hear from the world:

> One of the interesting things about success is that we think we know what it means. A lot of the time our ideas about what it would mean to live successfully are not our own. They're sucked in from other people...It is not that we should give up on our ideas of success, but that we should make sure that they are our own. We should...make sure that we own them, that we're truly the authors of our own ambitions.[4]

WE SAY "YES" TO DISTRACTIONS

The final gap is that learning to go for what we want requires us to say "yes" and "no" in the right ways. In other words, we need equal amounts of courage and willingness to start and stop doing the things that are required to make something different. Saying yes to new things is a bit more straightforward than saying no because there is always a bit of risk even with a polite turndown.

Vague "yes's" and "no's" are the by-products of unclear priorities, but "here's why" and "here's why not" are by-products of a clear line of sight.

However, we need the courage and willingness to say "no," draw a line in the sand, and avoid doing things that distract from our goals. To do this well, use language that goes beyond a simple "yes" or "no." Share your reasons "why" or "why not," and that will open up room for understanding and respect, regardless of the outcome. When the writer and cartoonist Hugh MacLeod said, "The best way to get approval is not to need it,"[5] he pointed to a very important element in our effort to create the change we want to see: be bold, then ask for permission.

CHAPTER SUMMARY

THE EFFECT

Your day has a plan for you, and the dilemma often has a mind of its own. The tasks, activities, and interruptive demands on your time and attention are a constant and direct challenge to the game plan you follow. Without a clear line of sight, you end up distracted from priorities and your higher objectives will always remain in a state of incompleteness.

THE HIDDEN INSIGHT

The clearest starting line is a visible finish line. However, just picking a point in the future and saying "I will accomplish X by this day" lacks context and a realistic reference point to the circumstances around you. When in the manager's dilemma, we often select (or inherit) goals and pursue them blindly, all the while acting surprised when unexpected challenges delay our progress or toss us off course entirely. Within the manager's dilemma, *we're wandering*, but once we discover our line of sight, *we start navigating*.

THE RESPONSE

Establishing a clear line of sight helps you make progress toward the things that matter to you. To create your picture, respond to four sequential questions:

1. What aspect of my work requires a greater level of alignment?
2. Within this area, what are all of the factors that matter to me and to others that I have to satisfy?
3. Which of these specific factors are important enough to track in my line of sight?
4. If any one of these factors fell away, what impact would that have on the outcomes and goals that this line of sight must produce?

THE SHIFT

A line of sight is more than just a list of your goals. It is a visible connection between your priorities, desired outcomes, and the factors that influence your pursuit of those things. When others are turned around or chasing their tails, you're tethered to a line of sight that sustains focus, direction, and progress toward what matters most to you. With a clear line to follow, you are ready to take the next step and *distinguish your contribution.*

Chapter 5

DISTINGUISH YOUR CONTRIBUTION

Because the dilemma knows how to keep you occupied with unimportant things that leave your distinctive value and impact on the sidelines

A DAY IN THE LIFE OF MANAGERS is marked by constant demands that push and pull them in many directions. Whether from bosses, peers, or direct reports, they are called upon to contribute in numerous, often conflicting, ways. The predominant effect of this scattered state is a diluted contribution with diminished impact both to the team and to the organization at large.

As the dilemma spreads us thinner, our efforts lose their impact, our already limited TERF is further thinned by the scattered approach, and our weakened results produce an even more limited contribution. When we are stuck in the dilemma, we can help but not be helpful. We can get things done, without moving priorities forward. We can execute other people's objectives without gaining personal value from the accomplishment.

We are only as vital as our contribution; so when the manager's dilemma spins our wheels and causes extra effort with less impact, we

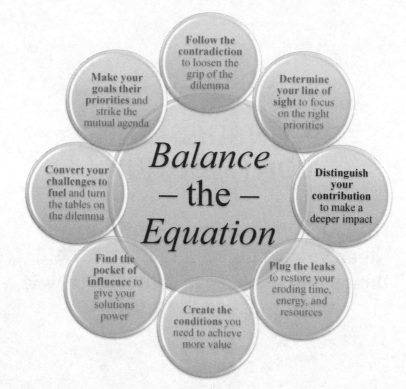

Figure 5.1 Distinguish your contribution.

have to push back by distinguishing our contribution and getting back to the *Performance Zone.*

As you begin to selectively deliver the right kind of value, you end up "helping less broadly" but influencing more deeply and with greater impact. When your contribution parallels your line of sight, you claim a distinct advantage from a more efficient use of your TERF. And fewer wasted efforts result in a surplus of available margin to draw upon when unexpected challenges and demands inevitably arise. This reversal from a vicious cycle to a virtuous cycle is your next critical move to *balance the equation.*

There are three core principles at the heart of what it means to *distinguish your contribution*: (1) when you negotiate with yourself, you're guaranteed to be on the losing end; (2) what you don't do is just as power-ful as what you do; and (3) being either overcommitted or undercommit-ted leads to underdelivering, but being *well-committed* gives you a chance to consistently deliver your best.

If you've been in a high-demand culture, then you're likely thinking: "Sounds good, but how can I do this when I rarely get the final say or when there are unwritten rules that everyone knows you just don't break if you want to advance?"

If factors like these are real for you, then you need to learn the art of *choosing, saying "yes,"* and *communicating "no."* This chapter is about learning to focus on and pursue the contribution that gives you the greatest chance to use your talent to succeed. Saying "yes" and align-ing your efforts with your priorities is about maintaining your line of sight. The ability to say "no" effectively has a lot to do with how you support people even when you decline to deliver specific contributions they request.

At the end of the day, it comes down to courage. The art of choosing, saying "yes" to yourself, and communicating "no" to others is your own small act of disruption. Nobody can or will do this for you, but being distinctive starts with your intentional distinctions and the willingness to make them real.

Your overall contribution is comprised of three related elements, including your *value-added capabilities, vital purpose*, and the *relevant results* you deliver.[1] Together, these three essentials are visible evidence of your personal brand, and they reflect the fundamental upside you bring to the table in your efforts to succeed in your role right now, as well as to stay relevant as you advance over time. However, the manager's dilemma has a way of lulling us into thinking that the best way to keep our heads above water is to stay in the action, do a little bit of everything, and say "yes" so that we appear willing and on board. This scramble blurs the edges of our purpose, capabilities, and results and separates us from our core capacity to influence in the best way possible.

THE BUSINESS CASE FOR YOU

Selective organizations and their leaders look to the strength of the "business case" before investing precious resources into new opportunities. Whether it concerns people, priorities, or projects, the business case includes a dispassionate and balanced assessment of the relative benefits, costs, and presumed impact of the potential choices. Essentially, it is the rational justification for saying "yes" or "no." One of the most important questions you can ask yourself is: *what's the business case for me in this organization*? If you are unable to answer the question with a compelling and evidence-based response, you may be at risk in your potential to remain on track in the career progression you seek.

"Everybody keeps piling more stuff to do on my plate, but why do their priorities have to be my emergency?" This common refrain among managers is a sign that they are delivering other people's contributions. A manager is just a commodity until they deliver their own distinctive value that produces a valued impact.

If you hear yourself rationalizing this question away with statements like "Of course I'm relevant; the organization will always need managers like me to do what I do...," then you need to know exactly how that sounds. It sounds like famous last words spoken the day before you got blindsided by something you could have anticipated if you had paid attention.

Your distinctive contribution is the business case for you in action. It is what helps you stand out, stay relevant, and get ahead of the change curve through consistent, value-driven performance. To avoid contribution-creep and determine a solid business case that compels leaders to say "yes" to you and continue investing their own time, energy, and resources in your development, start by defining your three interrelated components: *value-added capabilities, vital purpose*, and *relevant results*. Distinguishing these components will reconstitute your impact by concentrating your efforts around what matters most. It is one of the most reliable ways to quickly begin moving beyond the dilemma and elevate your personal brand in the process.

YOUR VALUE-ADDED CAPABILITIES

One of the most quietly debilitating effects of the manager's dilemma is the fact that it robs your solutions of their power. This means that the knowledge, skills, abilities, and managerial tools you have to solve problems are rendered ineffective when you do not have sufficient energy or focus to use them in the right way, at the right time.

Therefore, one of the leading requirements for successfully navigating your way out of the manager's dilemma is leveraging your specific, value-added capabilities—your individual solutions to meet the day-to-day challenges you face—in just the right ways consistently over time. Your capacity to do this sets you apart from other average contributors who dilute their value by doing too much with mediocre results. To begin, consider what's wrong with these statements?

- I'm a good people person.
- I like to solve big problems.
- I'm an excellent communicator.
- I get things done.

That was a trick question; there is nothing wrong with these statements if you are stuck in the manager's dilemma. These imprecise statements were the responses of people I've coached through the process of seeing how their diluted impact is watered down by their own vague understanding of their capabilities. These are the first takes and initial responses to the question: *Which of your contributions have the greatest value to your team and the organization?*

While in the manager's dilemma, we reach into a grab-bag of skills to meet any obligation that passes by us. Moving beyond it requires us to consistently draw upon a distinctive contribution of purpose, value, and impact and apply it in just the right ways. If you haven't thought about your contribution in this way before, try this exercise and simply finish each sentence:

- The strength that I rely upon most during challenging times is…
- The unique skill/talent I am most proud of is…
- The subtle but important impact I make on people is…

There really is no secret formula that will take you from these presenting, superficial statements to clear and precise definitions of your value-added contributions. It only requires a few repetitions to dig deeper, gain increasing insight, and express what you contribute in more concrete and specific terms. To make this clear, table 5.1 illustrates a progression from the initial statement to the finished version so you can see how several managers learned to distinguish their value. Following this example, there are multiple prompts that you can use to dig deeper on your own value-added capabilities in table 5.2.

Your value-added contributions can be framed as single skills or attributes, or they can merge together in a cluster of assets that are available to you in critical circumstances. That last part of the phrase is the key. For example, if you are able to "see the big picture and break it down into more manageable parts" to get it done, then that is a value-added contribution for sure. However, if what is needed by the organization is someone who can do that in crisis mode when things are under full pressure, then it is not a value-added capability if you can only deliver when you have time and predictability.

You have to know the skill and be able to use it when it counts for it to be a value-added capability. Using the blank grid in table 5.2, clarify your own top two:

Table 5.1 Clarify your value-added capabilities

First take: value-added capabilities	Clarified: value-added capabilities
I am a good people person.	I take time to build rapport with the people I work with. This allows me to customize my approach to every interaction. This little bit of forethought helps me avoid stepping on toes, and in the end I am more persuasive
I like to solve big problems.	My hand goes up when volunteers are needed for tough jobs. I thrive on the challenge, but more than that I am capable of taking a big-picture view and then breaking it down into manageable pieces
I am an excellent communicator.	I understand that communication is so much more than the words I say and the way I listen to others. I always take time to read the room in order to adjust my interactions in a way that gets something productive done. When the tone is crisis driven, I center myself and project a serious, but confident, presence. When things are light, I join in so people know they can relate to me
I get things done.	I work harder than most people, and my efforts go farther because I avoid distractions that can drain my energy. I don't flaunt it, but I let my boss and key colleagues know that things are delivered on time and above expectations

Table 5.2   Practice clarifying your value-added capabilities

First take: value-added capabilities	Clarified: value-added capabilities
Contribution #1:	
Contribution #2:	

YOUR VITAL PURPOSE

Your vital purpose is the single statement that describes why you are essential to the team and organization. It is not your title, nor is it a rehashed version of your most consistent achievements. The reality is that we have to transcend both of those superficial reference points. Your vital purpose expresses the critical role you play within your sphere of influence.

When well-crafted, purpose statements serve as a source of inspiration, guidance, and discipline for you to stay focused on what matters. They signal your fundamental impact on others and, although your actions will always have a greater effect than your words, you can use your purpose statement to subtly brand yourself in your team and the larger organization.

In order to do this, you must go from purpose statement, to *purpose profile*. Your profile is a reflection of the most productive combinations of vital purpose, value-added contributions, and related hidden challenges to watch out for. Before you craft your own, consider some of these examples from real managers:

Catalyst

Vital purpose: "I make things happen when nobody else can."

Valued capabilities: Catalysts are the sparks that make things happen. They think in innovative ways and their actions ignite progress when pressure and resistance build. Whether it is a subtle insight or a grand plan, catalysts have respect and use it to push ideas forward.

Hidden challenges: Bright, shiny objects can distract them from priorities and their impatience with structure can slow catalysts down. At times, they fail to ask enough of the right questions to identify important considerations, and they can be unreliable.

Producer

Vital purpose: "I get the job done, no matter how difficult the task."

Valued capabilities: Producers crank out lots of good work. They are focused on seeing what is needed to keep progress going, and they are skilled at following through on the delegation or completion of tasks. Smart, critical thinkers, producers can link strategy with execution effortlessly and although they prefer routine and structure, they remain flexible enough to adapt when needed.

Hidden challenges: Too much change in a short period of time can disrupt the cycle of implementation that producers need, which can frustrate them and reduce the quality of their work. They can be impersonal at times and forget about the importance of good relationships.

Look Out

Vital purpose: "I make the critical observations, insights, and connections that keep us out of trouble."

Valued capabilities: Look outs watch for bugaboos that can derail the show. They are compliance minded and often ask hard questions that create a helpful pause for necessary consideration. They see details that others don't, which enables them to assess opportunities and risks.

Hidden challenges: Look outs can get tunnel vision, make decisions too quickly, or fixate on potential risks that are actually acceptable to take on. This can create pessimism, resistance, and road blocks that prevent progress and frustrate others.

Truth Teller

Vital purpose: "I read the room and speak up at just the right time to say what needs to be said."

Valued capabilities: Truth tellers see it like it is and say it like it is. The invaluable perspective they bring can reveal dangerous gaps between ideas about what is possible and realities that limit it. When they speak their minds in ways that contribute positively, without offending people through excessive criticism, they help the team get to better results.

Hidden challenges: Truth tellers sometimes believe they have the "only" truth and may fail to listen to others. Their advocacy for singular perspectives (often based on personal biases) can alienate people and limit the expression of diverse viewpoints that are needed for healthy discussion and well-tested decisions.

Signal Caller

Vital purpose: "I keep people on the same page so that we achieve the goals that matter."

Valued capabilities: Signal callers are the quarterbacks that keep an eye on the coordination of roles and contributions. They are able to bring the best out of others because they understand that getting out of the way helps people stay on their vital purpose.

Hidden challenges: Signal callers can get distracted by their coordination efforts and fail to deliver their own skills and abilities to the task at hand. When they experience personal or professional adversity or high-pressure situations, they can be reactive and have difficulty engaging with others consistently enough to keep things moving. Signal callers need systems builders to create the structure for what needs to happen.

Systems Builder

Vital purpose: "I see the big picture, as well as the details required to put productive systems in place."

Valued capabilities: Systems builders understand the structure and function of getting work done, and they are able to translate ideas into action. They anticipate the mix of resources and capacity needed for producing high-quality outcomes, and they have the ability to see important interfaces between details and the big picture.

Hidden challenges: Systems builders can get caught up in the moving parts and minutiae of getting things done, which blocks their view of evolving conditions. Their dogged commitment to structure can some-times lead to black/white thinking that gets them stuck when more creative problem solving could address issues successfully.

Storyteller

Vital purpose: "I get people to understand and believe in something bigger than themselves."

Valued capabilities: Storytellers have a way of getting people on the same page by describing current scenarios and possible futures in ways that help people understand complex ideas. With powerful images, they translate the landscape around them in a way that encourages belief in what is possible. The connections between people and ideas that they communicate present a vision and a path forward that makes new initiatives more likely to succeed.

Hidden challenges: Storytellers can get captured by the drama and intrigue of their vision, which causes them to drift and overreach. They can get overly involved in work relationships at a personal level, which can lead to unchecked biases. Rather than communicating clearly, they sometimes emphasize the nuances and variations of a story in a way that confuses people and results in unclear options.

If you did not catch a glimpse of your unique combination of talent, experiences, and purpose in the examples here, use table 5.3 to create your own purpose profile from scratch. In column 1, try to name it with a headline "statement" and then draft a short, single-line description that captures the essence of your vital purpose. In column 2, you can transfer the work you just did clarifying your value-added capabilities in the last section of this chapter.

Table 5.3 Create your own purpose profile

My vital purpose	My valued capabilities	My hidden challenges

For hidden challenges, take an honest look at the recurring obstacles that you encounter as you try to stay on purpose and deliver your value. They could be the issues you face in your current circumstances, or they could be the problems you trigger when you use your value-added capabilities in excess.

YOUR RELEVANT RESULTS

At work, managers are measured by what they contribute. Your current performance reflects it, your access to better assignments and future advancement depend on it, and the quality of your working life is shaped by it. When you consistently deliver value to your team and organization, your contributions will always have a place because valued contributors have no expiration date. However, your inability to understand the underlying metric that converts capabilities and contributions into measurable results limits your opportunities for success. To do this, you have to keep your own scorecard, not so much as a broadcast tool, but as a real-time reference point to the results you produce.

Unfortunately, both a cause and compounding effect of the manager's dilemma is an interruption in our sustained results. Sometimes the interruption is abrupt and the precipitous fall in valued contribution is extreme. At other times, the decline can be slow as the things we do have steadily decreasing impact over time. In the former scenario, the effect is a failure to deliver results and we experience the immediate consequences that failure brings. In the latter, our results do not fall off the cliff as much as they just fade away.

When you are stuck in the dilemma, you have a tendency to think about outputs. For example, "I finally got all six of my overdue performance reviews completed." This statement reflects the mad scramble to produce quantity and to count that level of output as a meaningful result. But as we all know, there is a vast difference between the concepts of quantity and quality. Even more to the point, there is a difference between the outputs we count and the outcomes we create.

Outputs surely keep you busy, but outcomes are the markers of a distinctive contribution. An outcome is the measurable impact of the outputs we produce. Following the same example, here are important results framed as outcomes:

> I finally got all six of my overdue performance reviews completed... For one of my direct report who has been struggling to meet my minimum performance expectations I used the evaluation and subsequent face-to-face review to establish a greater level of urgency and a clearer set of accountabilities so he knows exactly where he stands. And, for my two top-performers, I developed specific development goals for each of them. We now have an agreement about how I will coach them to stay challenged and step up in their desired areas of growth. They both expressed similar feelings of gratitude about the opportunity and this may have prevented both of them from leaving to pursue other opportunities.

In this example, you can see that the manager's desired results had less to do with the number of outputs and more to do with the lasting outcomes from those efforts. Sure, outputs were necessary, but the outcomes that mattered to her had everything to do with moving an under-performing team member out of the organization and ensuring that no voluntary turnover occurred among her top performers.

If what is measured is what matters, then what are you measuring? This simple question requires a clear and precise answer. The following is a list of commonly defined outputs, which I frequently hear managers share in their effort to explain their results. In each example, notice how the task and activity described within the statement is valuable, but at the same time, it's too ambiguous to judge for relevant impact: build my team; motivate my people; set better direction; clarify our roles; communicate more openly; give better feedback; and evaluate individual performance more accurately.

In each of these examples, there is obvious superficial importance; however, the value is only recognizable when you dig inside the activity and pinpoint the concrete impact that elevates your contribution. In order to probe deeper for a more relevant result, simply give each

Table 5.4 Map your relevant results

My bosses expect…		I deliver on these
My bosses hold me		expectations by…
accountable for…		I measure them through…
	Up	
My peers expect…		I deliver on these
My peers judge me by…	*Across*	expectations by…
		I measure them through…
	Down	
My direct reports expect…		I deliver on these
My direct reports evaluate		expectations by…
me by…		I measure them through…

statement the "so that" test and follow where that leads you from outputs to measurable and relevant outcomes. For example, here is one that can actually include a quantifiable number to further measure the impact of the result: *Clarify our roles…* so that *we can eliminate the duplication of efforts and increase our team's overall productivity by 15 percent this fiscal year.*

In the next example, the qualitative experience is more important than the quantitative experience. However, the result is still relevant and measurable to a certain degree: *Communicate more openly…* so that *we can get dissenting ideas on the table to avoid brushing possible problems under the carpet and missing opportunities for innovation.*

In order to gain a more comprehensive view of your critical results, use the matrix in table 5.4 to define and plot out your outcomes up, down, and across your sphere of influence in your team and in the wider organization.

CHAPTER SUMMARY

THE EFFECT

The manager's dilemma spins our wheels, causing extra effort with less impact. At the very moment when we need our contributions to the team and organization to be at their best, the dilemma distracts us from priorities and lulls us into thinking that the best way to keep our heads above water is to do a little bit of everything.

THE HIDDEN INSIGHT

You can learn how to *contribute your way out* of the dilemma. Regardless of the pressures you face, you have to first control the choices you make about how you contribute. Otherwise, people and circumstances will dictate how and where you invest your time and energy. You can only do this by distinguishing your vital purpose, value-added capabilities, and the important results you deliver. If you do not know exactly what these things are, then who will?

THE RESPONSE

To avoid the dilemma's diluted contribution, spend time leveraging the key elements of yours. Look at the work you do; then dig deeper to name the vital purpose, value-added capabilities, and results that are the essential elements of your brand. To jumpstart the process, reflect on these prompts until you can confidently finish each sentence:

- The strength that I rely upon most during challenging times is...
- The unique skill/talent I am most proud of is...
- The subtle impact I make on people and projects is...

THE SHIFT

Rather than saying "yes" to every request, hone in on your distinctive contribution and be selective with the projects and priorities you accept to ensure alignment. This move synchronizes your assets and gives you leverage to perform better by keeping you in your sweet spot. When this happens, your impact is clearer and the recognition you receive for doing great work in your area of expertise produces more and better opportunities to shine. The contribution-creep caused by the manager's dilemma is thereby eliminated over time.

Chapter 6

PLUG THE LEAKS

Because the worst kind of problem is the one you don't know you have until it silently drains your resources and erodes the things you value

THE DILEMMA RELENTLESSLY PUNCHES small leaks into our already fragile TERF. These slow drips could be fixed in the moment with less time and effort; however, because we are overloaded and distracted by other concerns, we often fail to notice and address them. As leaks linger, they require an even greater effort to repair once the damage is done. Another classic dilemma calling card, the initial challenge of the leak is nothing compared to the compounding, secondary damage created by the delay in repairing it.

In technical terms, a leak is any *ongoing behavior, attitude, or action that reduces our performance*. In practical terms, leaks are those unwanted, recurring experiences that: (1) make it hard for us to get great work done; and (2) require an unbudgeted use of our TERF to address the inefficiencies they produce. In simpler terms, leaks are the annoying distractions, hurtful experiences, and unexpected challenges that unnecessarily drain us.

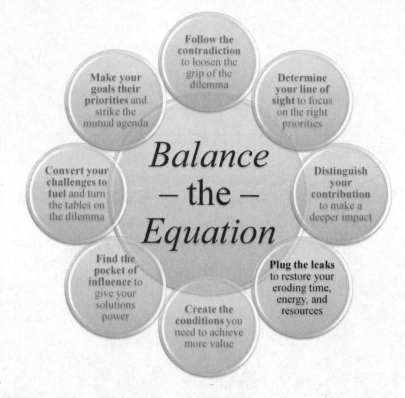

Figure 6.1   Plug the leaks.

Messes are an everyday part of our working lives, but they turn into leaks when we fail to clean them up early. Imagine that your working life is a house; there are some rooms that you don't visit as often as others because there is just too much ground to cover and too little time to do it. This is precisely what enables hidden corners to stay messy, neglected, and prone to sprout damaging leaks.

The good news is that most leaks are both recognizable and containable. With an ounce of focused attention we can proactively spot and repair them so that our available TERF is reserved for the bigger challenges we face. This is the final step you take to *balance the equation*. Once you stop the bleeding from those things that keep you inside the *Danger Zone*, you can *flip the scales* and really turn the tables on the dilemma. However, in order to build on what you accomplished by following the contradiction, determining your line of sight, and distinguishing your contribution you have to take the last step and *plug the leaks*.

In the Introduction I mentioned that some chapters are like field guides with actionable recommendations; this is one such chapter. The bulk of it includes examples that you can review now, then return to later as you experience the additional leaks I describe. The critical thing is to understand the ramifications of dilemma-sustaining leaks that concurrently threaten your productivity while draining your TERF. Once you grasp their importance, the insights and tools provided here can help you proactively address them.

The Dilemma Up Close: When you're stuck in the dilemma, you need rest and renewal, but you don't have the time to take it. You need to slow down and focus, but you're too busy to stop. You need to invest your highest energy and concentration on your top priorities, but you're spread thin and too depleted to concentrate. The reason you have no bandwidth to do these things is because your available TERF is drained by the distracting "leaks" that fritter away your capacity. Rather than using your time and energy to invest in what you value, the dilemma is a colander and your resources spill through the holes like water.

Janine was full of holes. It seemed like she couldn't go 15 minutes before another curveball or unexpected request showed up and caused another "minor" distraction. Just trying to keep up was an exhausting process; the problem was that her team was falling behind. Three months before this critical moment, she was asked to manage a group tasked with delivering an innovative service model for an important client. Without much experience with the new process, Janine was on a steep learning curve herself while she also had to rework the roles and project timelines. With a longer runway, she would have been fine. However, the first deliverable was already due the following Thursday at the close of business, and that's when her dilemma really kicked in.

The client called Monday at 9:30 a.m. to ask about the status of the project. By 11:45 p.m.—the time of the second phone call—the question changed to "why haven't you sent over the file?" Simply clarifying the agreed-upon delivery time of Thursday COB was apparently not enough. The calls continued throughout the day on Tuesday and Wednesday as well. This stress caused a ripple effect, and her team began to second guess their efforts. While they were well-meaning, every time Janine had to calm someone down or reiterate the game plan more precious time and energy was spent.

By Wednesday morning, her team's work was done; however, Janine now had to wait for her two bosses to review and approve the work before she could send it to the client. This meant that she was now feeling the pressure in three dimensions: the client's well-intentioned but harassing behavior frayed her last nerves; her team's constant check-ins drained her remaining composure; and seeing the files sit idly on her bosses' desks (a sign of their comfort with last-minute action) only increased her anxiety. Janine was caught in the middle as the last of her TERF drained away. After coaching Janine through the experience, I asked her to tell me what she learned. She said:

When expectations weren't clear, every gap took time to address. When it came down to the wire there was just no extra time or energy to spare. Anytime we stopped to talk about things or tweak somebody's role we spent a lot of energy re-grouping, but most of the switches were unnecessary anyway. I need to clarify roles and communicate with my team better from the start.

And next time, before the clock starts ticking so loudly, I will manage up better by establishing clearer expectations with my bosses. Their slow review of the work really stressed me out, but it could have been avoided if I expressed the full picture to them. Rather than just "handling things myself," I need to share more details about what's going on. Although the deliverable was technically not late, each phone call signaled that our important client wasn't happy. Much of my worry and wasted effort was preventable; I just needed to plug the leaks to reserve my capacity for when I need it most!

DO YOU HEAR THAT DRIPPING SOUND?

Leaks show up in diverse and subtle forms, which is part of what makes them difficult to spot. For over a decade now, I have painstakingly mapped hundreds of examples that threaten our learning and performance, as well as the quality of our working lives. There are too many to name here, so I chose a few of the most common dilemma-driven drips to highlight.

To simplify things, you will learn about two types of leaks that are prominent within the manager's dilemma. First, there are *visible leaks* that disrupt our flow and require a short-term use of TERF to regroup and get back on track. I refer to these visible leaks as *Pings, Zings*, and *Dings*. Their names fit their crimes, and as you will see, these leaks are easily repaired once we know how to look and listen for them.

> Like leaky pipes under a sink, the first repair is the busted plumbing; but then there is the collateral damage from standing water. The obvious challenge with leaks is that they go largely undetected until after the secondary damage escalates.

The second category includes *unseen leaks* that silently deplete us. These are hazardous both because of their stealth and because of the inefficient habits and patterns of behavior that we take on to work around them. Like any leak, the unseen variety produces a harsher double negative that bleeds bandwidth in a shorter period of time.

One reason the dilemma lingers is because it forces us to focus exclusively on what's right in front of us. When we see only the presenting side of our experience, that is, the fire of the day and so on, we fail to witness the subtler things. Plugging the visible and unseen leaks that fuel and sustain your manager's dilemma requires you to look beyond the distractions in front of you and start checking the closets and cabinets.

VISIBLE LEAKS: PINGS, ZINGS, AND DINGS

Every day brings a variety of pings, zings, and dings. These are the visible leaks that we hear, see, and feel more or less when they occur. While they do not diminish the challenges they bring, these are easier to address because of the fact that they occur much closer to the surface of our everyday experience.

The Dilemma Up Close: Allison, a member of my team, was struggling to find quiet time to focus on a project that required concentration and precise writing. The ringing phone and friendly "drop-bys" at her office were such a distraction that she took desperate measures. One day around 2:00 p.m. I went to check in with her only to find her office empty. The room had a clear view of the parking lot, and in a passing glance, I saw her sitting in her car. She was wearing headphones and typing furiously on her laptop, which was propped on the steering wheel. You can run but you can't hide from *Pings*!

PINGS

Pings are *minor distractions that require quick considerations*. For example, just when you get into the flow of a task, someone interrupts to "get your thoughts" on an unrelated issue. Perhaps a colleague stops by for an informal chat, or maybe one of your direct reports needs critical direction as a deadline looms. Of course, we also think of technology with a word like "ping," which has slowly become a preferred noun, verb, and adjective in the digital age. We get pinged by email, voicemail, text messages, calendars requests, and other forms of real-time communication. Without discipline and organization in our response habits, pings can keep our head on a swivel and our attention span even narrower than usual.

As a one-time occurrence, pings are just a normal part of our interconnected world of work. They are points of intersection between people and projects, and they are the communication pathways that move us along in our process to get work done. However, pings turn into leaks when "they happen to us," and the constant sidetracking knocks us out of the driver's seat, leaving us suspended in their distraction. To give you some examples to help you spot your own, here are a few of the most common pings I see, including a little "tape and glue" to plug them:

Description: "The unexpected request from a boss" can throw your day way off course. Ideally, these demands match our priorities, but they often do not. When we drop everything for other people, we're left to pick up the pieces.

Tape and glue: If the request is not in your line of sight or aligned with your desired contribution, then say no if at all possible. If no is not an answer you can give, negotiate the timing as best you can without compromising your flow.

Description: "The negative coworker" who thinks the sky is falling, nothing is fair, and that everyone is out to get them is an annoying leak. Just when you are decidedly *not* in the mood, they have a way of finding you, bending your ear, and exhausting you with their repetitive grievances.

Tape and glue: Whether it is out of politeness, indecision, or absurd amusement, we often let this leaker run wild. But you have to rip the band-aid off and say (as politely as you wish), "Now is not a good time for this conversation." Don't feed the trolls, period.

Description: "Ineffective collaboration" that wastes time and produces inferior results drains your TERF fast and hard. Although partnering with others is an essential ingredient of accomplishing large-scale change, not all collaboration is worth trying.

Tape and glue: Instead of collaborating out of convenience or obligation, be selective when it comes to when, how, and with whom you partner. Intentional partnering maximizes the chance of success by aligning the necessary resources with the essential contributors in the best way.

Description: "The sounds of technological intrusions" are the most common pings. That little noise or visible "pop up window" lets you know when someone wants your attention and whether you are concentrating on a task or not. These pings can derail your focus easily and often.

Tape and glue: If you are distracted by these electronic trapdoors, turn them off, hit "do not disturb," or log out. The more proactively you communicate, the less intense the search will be when you've gone missing for the 15 minutes that others think was an eternity.

ZINGS

Zings are those *surprise criticisms that cause quick reactions*. It does not matter what the other person's intentions were; if we feel zinged, then it qualifies. Whether it was an exchange of feedback gone wrong, or just a poorly worded message that inadvertently offends, these can have minor impacts or they can leave damaging effects on relationships where there is insufficient trust or commitment for the repair. Sometimes you ask for the regular, but they still give you the spicy mustard!

With zings, there are two common types of reactions. Depending on our preferences and tendencies, we may withdraw or we may confront the oncoming zinger with one better. If we have experience, training, and practice, then perhaps we respond in an assertive manner that addresses our thoughts and feelings without personalizing it, attacking the other person, or making the situation worse by escalating the tension. However, most of us are pretty imperfect when it comes to zings, so when we get that left-handed compliment or experience the passive/aggressive interaction, it quickly becomes a leak.

We spend precious TERF either nursing the hurt feelings as we brood silently at work, then at home later, then back at work the next day wishing we would have *said this* or *done that*. Alternatively, if we aggressively responded to the situation, then we are left with some damage control and relationship repair that is required to get things back on track. Here are some of the most common zings I observe:

Description: When "someone goes above your head" without working with you first, it cuts you out at the knees. Depending on the situation, it can feel like a minor embarrassment or a larger hit to your credibility.

Tape and glue: Address it head on by initiating a conversation and showing your cards. If you felt disrespected, then let them know, but listen for their reasons too. Look for the quickest way to establish a new expectation and move on.

Description: "Getting cut-off, interrupted, or strong-armed" by a colleague can leave you feeling unimportant and dismissed. One of the least collaborative gestures, this kind of steamrolling is a shutdown move that can make you question the point of future cooperation.

Tape and glue: Unless you want to escalate the situation, don't match aggression with aggression. If you have a meaningful contribution to make, continue to elevate that perspective. The more calmly (and assertively) you name the situation, the worse the offender looks.

Description: The "passive/aggressive criticism" that a colleague sends your way in a meeting not only zings, but it's hard to confront because the indirectness leaves room for interpretation.

Tape and glue: Without snark, and with your calmest demeanor and most neutral tone, ask: "Can you clarify that point; I wasn't sure what you meant?"

Description: When "someone else takes the credit for something you produced," it zings to the core. Whether the person inadvertently accepts the praise or honestly didn't see your contribution, the sting lasts until you find a way to gain the rightful recognition for what you achieved.

Tape and glue: Nobody wants to raise a petty hand to say, "I helped too!" But if there is a chance to set the record straight in a professional way right then and there, by all means do it. If not, initiate a conversation with key people to openly discuss your contribution and impact.

DINGS

Finally, dings are the *surprise challenges that disrupt your flow* and leave deeper cuts in your TERF. Although pings and zings are challenging, these can be much worse.

For example, when you inaccurately estimate how much time it will take for a project and you inadvertently overcommit yourself, you get dinged by your failure to follow through. When you've diligently worked on a project for months, only to get blindsided when the decision above you was made to cancel the effort, you get dinged. When a once-friendly colleague abruptly breaches the trust you had, you get dinged. When you receive a delayed performance evaluation with vague feedback that leaves you little time to address it, you get dinged. When the tactics of the leaders around you conflict with your values, the rift is a ding that's hard to reconcile.

In each of these examples, the leakiness occurs when we spend time processing, working around, or plowing through the unexpected challenge. Whether our progress is suddenly swept away by seemingly arbitrary changes or we just get a little beat up by the people and conditions around us, dings are disruptive and damaging leaks that sustain the dilemma. Here are some of the most common dings I observe:

Description: "Being overlooked for an opportunity" that you wanted can cause a deep, hard-to-recover-from ding. Whether it was a promotion or spot on a new project team you coveted, working hard and feeling qualified only to be turned away is impossible not to take personally.

Tape and glue: Whether there are good reasons, believable reasons, or unacceptable reasons, we can hold a grudge and let the loss change us, or we can define ourselves in another way. The glue is to rediscover your motivation, channel it into a new objective, and choose to move on.

Description: "Receiving influential feedback without the opportunity to address it" can feel like a major breach of trust. It destabilizes your relationship to the people involved and it undermines confidence in your standing. It is one thing to get critical feedback, but another to be dinged with it and not have the opportunity to respond before the consequences are felt.

Tape and glue: To move forward, you have to have a serious and direct conversation with the feedback giver as quickly as possible so the effects do not reach further than they need to. This includes an honest assessment about the relevant input, as well as a separate but related conversation (and new expectation for the future) about the way it was delivered.

Description: "Being blamed for a failure" that had other causes and drivers is a ding that is almost too tough to recover from, but you can when you own your part and separate the rest.

Tape and glue: The tricky part is that you don't want to look like you are deflecting blame or scapegoating, but at the end of the day you have to stand up for yourself and call it like you see it.

Description: "Self-inflicted dings" from counterproductive behaviors drain our TERF in serious ways. Five common "nots" include: (1) not trusting yourself, (2) not relying on the support of others, (3) not following through on priorities, (4) not pushing yourself to risk more, and (5) not letting go of past disappointments.

Tape and glue: We are our toughest critics, and there is nothing more scathing than thinking we "should have done something" that we knew was right. To plug these "not" leaks, let it go immediately, and commit this mantra to memory: "I trust myself, I rely on others, I follow-through on what matters, and I risk falling down."

As you can see from the scope of these examples, pings, zings, and dings reflect a diverse range of our challenging experiences managing people, projects, and priorities. But while these everyday disruptions are difficult, they are the types of leaks that can be eliminated with a little time and focused effort. However, the leaks that have real staying power and lasting effect are the *unseen leaks* that affect "*how we work*," not just "*what we're working on*" at the moment.

UNSEEN LEAKS

The remaining portion of this chapter is devoted to naming some of the most common unseen leaks. I have grouped them in "individual" and "team" categories, though the boundaries are often blurry. The examples flag the major individual and team leaks while providing a starting point to plug them with *tape and glue*.

LEAKS *FROM* INVISIBLE LEADERSHIP

Description: When you are stuck in the manager's dilemma, you simply cannot be everywhere and fully present all the time. While you may not intend to drop off the face of the earth, the dilemma has a way of consuming you and bringing on periods when you are simply unavailable to other people. When "attention to other priorities" turns into unintentional disengagement— regardless of whether it is justified in some way—the leak can derail the good things you have going with your team.

Typical punctures: When we disappear at the very moment our people need us, we trigger leaks that stem from communication gaps, redundant efforts, missed deadlines, and inconsistent accountabilities. The face of these punctures can be seen in the three primary effects of invisible leadership: (1) When people cannot see you show up in the face of difficult situations, they cannot trust you—so be present and engage. (2) When people cannot hear you when they need direction, they cannot follow you—so share what you think is important. (3) Finally, when people cannot feel that you appreciate and respect their contribution and effort during difficult times, they cannot stand up for you—so give them what you want to receive.

Tape and glue: Here are three important steps managers can take to plug the leak through proactive choices and behaviors:

1. Make *values* visible—Talk about what matters, share your point of view about the underlying factors that influence your decisions and behaviors, and invite others to do the same.

2. Make *priorities* visible—Make crystal clear the priorities that matter above others, work together to negotiate goals and objectives to maximize the contributions from others, and remain transparent when conditions change to avoid frustration and disappointment.

3. Make *communication* visible—Rather than relying on minimal efforts to communicate, use multiple channels even at the risk of overcommunicating. Combine the email with the hallway conversation, and add a face-to-face team meeting to supplement the one-to-one conversations that already occurred.

LEAKS *FROM* CONSTANT CRISIS FATIGUE

Description: When comfortably established in the *Performance Zone*, we are well positioned to deal with everyday challenges and adversity. With a healthy margin, we are more likely to maintain our perspective, take time to consider options, and respond quickly with proactive decisions that make the best of challenging circumstances. However, when our margin wanes and we tilt toward the *Danger Zone*, adversity can ignite the dilemma and force us into a constant crisis mode that distorts our perspective on the challenge at hand and makes its negative effects reach further and last longer than necessary.

Typical punctures: Once inside the *Danger Zone*, the flashpoint of an issue can easily send us into reaction mode where we stop thinking critically and lose sight of our capacity to influence the situation. When we get caught in a reactionary mode, every crisis has at least two phases. First, there is the disruptive event and the actual damage that it causes. Then there is the impact from the "reaction" to the event itself. When we do not respond effectively to the first phase, we add collateral damage (because of our ineffective response) to the initial adversity. In other words, every crisis lasts longer and causes more damage than it needs to.

Tape and glue: To address urgent situations once and comprehensively, the following framework provides a detailed flow to regain momentum and productively work through the challenge:

- *establish* a comprehensive picture of the current situation;
- *integrate* diverse perspectives to see the full picture;
- *align* people around the top issues and priorities;
- *leverage* specialized expertise and knowledge to determine necessary change;
- *develop* shared ownership of the solutions; and
- *extend* momentum past the flashpoint to enable long-term collaboration.

LEAKS *FROM* PERFECTIONISM

Description: While perfectionism can be an admirable trait in principle, the excessive search for the highest and greatest results is a leak that impedes your performance. Perfectionist behaviors that seek to control experience require a high degree of predictability, which is not a hallmark of the world in which we work. This pursuit makes us more rigid and less likely to admit failure and risk learning new things, both of which are keys to adaptability and development.[1]

Typical punctures: These leaks are visible when mounting to-do lists pile up because things are never finished "enough" (unless they are perfect, which is rare for a true perfectionist). As the excessive focus on polish detracts from the substance, progress slows and people get frustrated. This not only prevents work from getting done, but it can inadvertently create the impression that your collaborators aren't good enough.

Tape and glue: To repair this leak implement the following actions:

- *maintain* realistic expectations for finished products;
- *design* work flows that prioritize substance over polish;
- *distinguish* between excellence and perfection; and
- *accept* a basic level of uncertainty.

LEAKS *FROM* SELF-HANDICAPPING

Description: This leak shows up when we unconsciously sabotage ourselves by setting unattainably high goals, taking on too much at once, or procrastinating by focusing on other priorities. These self-handicapping actions precipitate failure and undermine our effectiveness, while conveniently leaving us room to point to other causes of the breakdown.[2]

Typical punctures: When this kind of leak is present, it is accompanied by declining confidence and mounting frustration. These *Danger Zone* characteristics are more likely to produce missed deadlines, give rise to unmet accountabilities, and reduce trust among colleagues.

Tape and glue: Implement realistic goal setting and engage proactively with supporters to get feedback on feasibility, timing, and other factors that are required for success. Rather than focusing on prior failures, focus on setting up better opportunities to succeed in the future.

TEAM LEAKS

LEAKS *FROM* INDECISION

Description: There are a variety of subtle, but powerful factors that reduce our ability to make timely decisions. When a state of "indecision" takes hold, the manager's dilemma pins you in a corner and keeps you burning energy without covering any ground. If you have ever set aside an important decision, then you know that there can be some good reasons to step away. If we are intentional, then we might use the time to gather information and reflect on the choice at hand. However, when we get into avoidance mode, we run the risk of missing windows of opportunity and letting decisions linger in ways that take a toll through the burden of indecision.

Typical punctures: Simply put, the same decisions have to be made and remade because the lack of conviction and follow-through cause false starts and delays. Whether for good reasons or not, these intermittent delays lead to a "treadmill" effect where priorities are pursued, then derailed by distraction, then pursued again as time, energy, and resources are slowly drained by each successive effort to move forward.

Tape and glue: The best way to plug the leak is to identify the type of indecision, understand why we do it, and then simply *stop*. Table 6.1 explains some of the common types of indecision I see among managers stuck in the dilemma.

LEAKS *FROM* UNHEALTHY COMPETITION

Description: Unhealthy internal competition results in split allegiances and mutually exclusive goal attainment. When there is too much competition, people work against each other in both overt and covert ways. The net result of leaks like this are a decrease in information sharing, effective collaboration, and joint problem-solving that work together to undermine positive team virtues such as loyalty, open information sharing, and innovation.

Table 6.1   Leaks from indecision

Indecision	Definition	Why we do it
The escape hatch	Deciding on a course of action with an obvious "out" to avoid follow through	It's the best of both worlds; we do it and don't have to do it all at the same time
The treadmill	A never-ending cycle of deciding, but never being fully decided	We never have to commit, and we get to sidestep the guilt of "avoiding" the issue
The stall	Finding a shelf and sticking all of the possible choices on top of it, out of reach	We get to look at our options from afar, separating ourselves from the pressure
The blinders	Brazen and bold, this is deciding not to decide knowing full well what's at stake	We trigger ourselves into a kind of survival mode that justifies avoidance

Typical punctures: If one of us wins and one of us loses, the natural leak produces a quick decline in information sharing. Why would I offer my good ideas when I do not trust relationships based on a win/lose mentality? Left unchecked, this mindset pervades decision-making and team goals are diminished in light of individual goals. Over time it leads individuals to censor themselves and create mindguards where innovative thinking is inhibited.

Tape and glue: To quickly plug the leak and reverse the erosion of open communication, effective collaboration, and necessary innovation, ensure there is no performance/reward disconnect that leaves people feeling trapped to either "compete or fail." Once there is neutral or positive incentive to work together, establish expectations that great ideas can come from anywhere, recognize the contributions of others, and encourage an atmosphere of creative dissent that allows people to speak truthfully about what works and doesn't work in ways that do not associate criticism with individual performance.

LEAKS *FROM* UNFINISHED BUSINESS

Description: The worst kind of leak is the one that is deeply rooted in your everyday routine and therefore is difficult to notice and even harder to shift. One such leak, caused by the constant rushing and corner cutting of the dilemma, is the unfinished business left over from hurried conversations, truncated meetings, and hastily written emails. When there is always another discussion, meeting, or message to attend to, we convince ourselves that half-hearted attempts are the best we can do. Seeking premature closure due to pressure from deadlines, fatigue, or difficult issues can leave important work started, but not finished. The result of this permanence tendency is that staff meetings end without resolution, discussions start and end with no closure, and problems are partially resolved, but not fully addressed.[3]

Typical punctures: The leak shows up as frustration from lack of closure, disengagement in meetings that feel endless because things never sunset, conversations that are left dangling because what needs to be said has not been said, and other forms of partial communication that tell part of the story but not all of it. The growing sense of burnout for people on this merry-go-round of constant problem chasing only compounds the dilemma's drain of your TERF.

Tape and glue: To plug the leak, make investments of time and energy that match the need at hand. Rather than looking for quicker conversations and shorter meetings, take as much time as needed to get the right things done right. If closure is not achieved, agree on a clear next milestone that will facilitate it in a reasonable amount of time. Finally, get energized from successfully resolving issues and achieving priorities so that the anticipation is shared to get things to the finish line.

CHAPTER SUMMARY

THE EFFECT

The dilemma punches small leaks into our already fragile TERF. This is a key element of its "disorient and disable" effect. Because we often fail to notice and address leaks, they silently linger and our neglect requires an even greater effort to repair once greater damage is done. As managers we organize our behavior around the beliefs we hold, so if we believe that "small, inconvenient, and annoying" leaks are unimportant, then we create workaround patterns that only sustain the trickle and elevate their adverse impact. Recognizing that all leaks matter because of their TERF draining effects is the final step toward balancing the equation.

THE HIDDEN INSIGHT

Some leaks are visible the moment they spring, while others are unseen and harder to discover. The visible leaks are easier to detect when encountered, but the unseen leaks become embedded more deeply into our routines and have a tendency to stick around much longer. In order to plug both types of the leaks, we have to readjust our mindset from reaction to prevention, and then proactively pursue them.

THE RESPONSE

The capacity to spot and repair leaks quickly helps us to balance the equation and regain the full use of our TERF. To plug your leaks, pinpoint the drip (any time frustration mounts and progress is blocked) and follow where it leads. Once you see it in the light of day, take your time to consider the source, reflect on the causes, get others involved as needed to take action, and then recheck to confirm the patch.

THE SHIFT

Ironically, even when we stumble upon an emerging leak early, it can lull us into believing that it's okay to ignore it—after all, "it's just a little drip, how bad could it be?" But by the time you square up to face a slow leak, the damage has already been done. The shift toward balance is an aggressive search for and response to any leak that unnecessarily drains your capacity. The result is a fuller restoration of your TERF and the increase in efficiency you gain when those old, leaky pipes are finally repaired.

You won't find a reference to these pages in the table of contents. In the same way the manager's dilemma brings unexpected challenges to trip you up, here are a few hidden insights to help you go from balancing the equation *to* flipping the scales.

When it comes to horrible curses, the tragic figure of Sisyphus got a gnarly one. As punishment for his deceitfulness, he was forced to roll a huge boulder up a hill each day, only to watch it roll down again. The punishment required him to repeat this futile task every day for eternity. In one story, you feel like the condemned character of Sisyphus. Work is your curse, and the endless, self-defeating task of rolling the boulder is punishment meted out by the manager's dilemma.

But in another story, you turn the tables on the dilemma. In this version, something else beyond the frustrating monotony is possible. You're no longer a victim of the forces that lie outside of your control; instead, you're an astute observer of them, and you watch for their seams and cracks so you can manipulate the openings to your advantage. When this more powerful story gains traction, you outsmart the dilemma with strategies that undermine the very traps it uses to keep you indefinitely rolling the boulder up the hill. The four strategies you just learned to balance the equation provide the spark of inspiration you need to make this new story real.

In a way, our stories are like maps and they reveal where we are, where we're not, and what features must be negotiated to move in a given direction. To navigate your way out of the dilemma with intention, you need to become a cartographer, though I could argue that you already are. For example, think about managing another person's work and the concept of *story maps* becomes crystal clear.

For each team member, you provide information about the organization and their important objectives (i.e., you help them get a lay of the land); establish their performance requirements (i.e., you pinpoint their destination and the likely routes they'll take to arrive there); and communicate regularly to check progress and required adjustments (i.e., you use the map's legend to interpret the unique features they encounter along the way). When someone says, "I can't seem to get over the hump on this issue," they're saying they misread the incline of the terrain. When a team member says, "I feel a little turned around on this project," they're saying that they no longer have their orientation within the map.

As any manager knows, the mapmaker has tremendous power to get people aligned and moving in the same direction, or *not* if they fail to accurately communicate it. We make maps for other people all of the time, but what kind of map guides you?

Whatever your picture is, it begins with the story you tell about the journey you're on right now. The final four chapters will open new destinations, which are otherwise inaccessible, when the story you believe has you stuck in the dilemma rolling heavy boulders up endless hills.

PART 3

FLIP THE SCALES

As you follow the contradiction, determine your line of sight, distinguish your contribution, and plug the leaks that hinder your performance and drain your TERF, you rebalance the inverse equation of shrinking resources and increasing demands. But just getting back to level ground is not an indicator of success. If you want to fundamentally alter the situation, then you need something more radical. To go beyond the dilemma, you have to *flip the scales*. This requires four strategic moves that render the dilemma's effects irrelevant. Over time, they will restore your influence and tilt you out of the *Danger Zone* and move you back into your *Performance Zone*.

Chapter 7

CREATE YOUR CONDITIONS

Because knowing *what to do* and even *how to do it* is not enough: You have to know how to generate the required circumstances to make it all happen

THE HECTIC PACE OF THE MANAGER'S dilemma can make us think things are random, but behind every experience and outcome there is always a set of specific conditions that made it possible. The dilemma delivers unwanted conditions that undermine our capacity to achieve what we want, but to flip the scales you have to intentionally craft your own.

Learning how to create the conditions you need is a powerful way to align your big-picture goals with the day-to-day interactions required to achieve them. This begins with a shift in focus from accomplishments to conditions.

The Dilemma Up Close: It was 11:45 p.m. on Thursday and Becky was exhausted but satisfied with her efforts to prime the event for success. She could not have worked harder, double-checked her to-do lists more frequently, or managed the project better from a technical perspective.

Figure 7.1   Create your conditions.

She anticipated a successful conference the following day, and she had every reason to trust in that expectation, but things fell apart in a big way the next morning. It was not a minor disappointment where things could have been a bit smoother; it was an embarrassing gaffe that disrupted the event from the start and ultimately lost her the client account.

I worked with Becky, a successful corporate event designer, in the aftermath of this extremely difficult situation. She wanted to know why things went off the rails in such an unexpected way. As an experienced manager in charge of high-profile client events, she had never really stumbled. Her approach to work was marked by a relentless focus on tracking every detail and accomplishing each sequential task at all stages of the planning process. Nothing got missed, and this style worked well for her, up until now. So she wondered what happened and *why she couldn't see it coming?*

Although she didn't know it at the time, Becky was caught in the manager's dilemma. Her team's portfolio of client events was 15 percent greater than the prior year (which was already a record for her) and the complicated travel calendar bumped her stress level to near breaking point. Adding to the complexity and change, Becky had a new assistant producer, Brad, who joined the team two months before. Despite these changes and increased responsibilities, she was a "pro's pro," and her determination and work ethic still had her on track for a successful conference.

As I talked with Becky, I recognized a fair, meticulous, and demanding manager. When I asked her to describe her approach to communicating with the team, she explained:

> *Everyone has a job to do and I expect them to do it. I do not call meetings frequently but of course people know that I have an open door. My management style is to let everyone have the space to get their work done. After all, we are busier than we have ever been and there is frankly no time to waste and no margin for error.*

Recognizing that the general theme of collaboration would be an important aspect of her leadership development, I set that aside for the time being to explore the immediate factors that contributed most directly to the failure. First, I pointed out one of the dilemma's paradoxical beliefs that was embedded in her thinking (i.e., there is no margin for error, yet no time to stay on the same page), which made her prone to leaks. In addition to this, there was *the hectic schedule that placed borderline unrealistic expectations on the team, the minimal communication channels available to address contingencies,* and *the absolute focus on getting tasks checked off the countdown calendar without watching the big picture.*

The issue that derailed the event involved a slide with incorrect data that the president of the company inadvertently read in her opening remarks from the stage. The crushing aspect of the error was that Brad actually recognized the possibility of a glitch during the cue-to-cue rehearsal

Friday night. In the walk-through, he noticed that the first three slides had old formatting, which meant the content itself could be old too. However, the company's content expert was unavailable, and the president was already late for another interview and couldn't remain on stage for the rehearsal any longer. As Becky was completely enmeshed in other details, Brad chose to move past the contradiction, wrap up the rehearsal, and move on to the next priority.

The choice not to speak up or take steps to ensure accuracy caused a chain reaction: the president read the inaccurate financial numbers during the live show; the audience reacted poorly; and, in the aftermath, Becky's team was held responsible in an effort to help the client save face internally.

Clearly, nobody wanted anything bad to happen, nor did they intentionally sabotage the event. In fact, when the details were discovered, Becky did not blame Brad. She understood the pressure Brad was under and the fact that he made an undesirable choice in a lose-lose situation: one fire was avoided in order to move ahead and put a different one out. Seeing this impossible situation was one of the biggest breakthroughs for Becky.

Earlier in our discussion Becky identified one of her greatest strengths as "the capacity to track countless details and organize the right sequence of work." To contrast this, I asked her to respond to this question: Generally speaking, what are the ingredients of a successful event? Not so much from a technical standpoint, but what does your team need to do in order to coordinate their efforts to make the event a success? She answered:

> We have to have precision. With highly produced meetings like these everything is scripted down to the second. Things always come up, so we have to be able to adapt on the fly. And our roles all touch the others in some way so we have to be able to trust each other, communicate clearly, and then move on quickly after setbacks.

After she named these elements, I explained to Becky that these factors are the underlying conditions required for her team's success. In fact, her job as a manager is all about establishing the right environment where these success factors exist and her team can leverage them to produce outstanding events with great results for her clients. To be sure things were crystal clear, I asked Becky if she could envision a successful, high-stakes event that her team could produce where these conditions did not exist. She simply said *"No, and that was the problem!"*

For Becky, this was the moment she discovered what she already knew. She was a smart, talented, and successful manager, but the dilemma had pushed her to focus exclusively on getting the job done. The checklists and activity spreadsheets were important, but they only added real value when the required element of teamwork was already in place.

Owning this responsibility, Becky committed to spend more time check-ing in with each team member. She wanted to ask better questions and create a learning environment that would convert small mistakes into valued discussion points in order to avoid the big one. Her plan was not only to engage, but to listen for the subtle challenges her team encoun-tered to determine if there was a missing condition that would under-mine its success.

Like Becky, we all focus on accomplishing the tasks and activities on our overflowing to-do lists. But managers cannot afford to think only about the details of final outcomes. They have to consider the condi-tions that are required for their desired success to be achieved.

FROM ACCOMPLISHMENTS TO CONDITIONS

For some very good reasons—whether it is to "catch up" by stemming the tide of overflowing priorities, or to "get ahead" by proactively mov-ing the ball down the field—we incessantly rush to get things done. However, in true dilemma fashion, there is a nasty shadow effect to this outwardly positive trait. What appears to be a good thing is actually one of the greatest TERF wasting traps that sustain the dilemma's hold.

In our hasty pursuit of finished tasks and completed priorities, we naturally focus on the endpoints of our goals. As a result, we fail to consider "what comes first," and we overlook the fact that any potential achievement requires a dynamic set of underlying conditions that make it possible. In Becky's case, the team required the ability *to adapt on the fly, trust each other, communicate clearly*, and *move on quickly after setbacks*.

In other words, her ability to foster conditions of *flexibility, transparency*, and *resilience* was the primary driver of the team's success. Regardless of how technically sound she and others were in their jobs, it was the presence of influential factors like these that made it either *more* or *less* likely that the desired outcomes of the event would materialize.

Part II of this book provided four strategies to help you balance your inverse equation of shrinking resources and increasing demands. With that extra room to breathe, this chapter takes you further upstream—away from the point of experience—to teach you how to create the flexible conditions that better withstand unexpected challenges and make success possible.

> The dilemma causes you to focus on smaller and smaller things. Eventually, this erodes the perspective you have on the "big picture" and leaves you racing to stay busy, but not productive and to stay in motion, without going anywhere important. *Individual contributors can have to-do lists, but managers need* condition lists *because rapid change and increasing complexity require a more strategic type of action.*

Most of us can live with the frustration that comes along with an honest mistake or with simply being outplayed by a worthy competitor. But as Becky found out, it is difficult to live with the frustration that comes when we work hard, do everything "right," and still come up short. Getting blindsided by that unexpected challenge or unforeseen risk is frustrating because it not only sets us back from achievement we needed, but it leaves us with fewer resources for our other goals left waiting in the wings. Because they are malleable, conditions offer us a defense against unexpected changes that can derail our efforts.

If you want to win the new business with a stellar presentation, then you need to create the conditions for *focused preparation* and *confident execution*. If you want to turn that resistant team member into an engaged champion, then you need to create the conditions of *personal connection* and *motivation*. If you want to show that senior leader what you are truly capable of doing, then you need to create conditions of *visibility* and *advocacy*. Finally, if you want to develop the courage to say "no" to things that do not match your values, then you need to create the conditions of *clarity* and *commitment* to say "yes" to the right things. To unpack the concept of creating your conditions, the following Q&A simplifies the main points.

WHAT'S WRONG WITH FOCUSING ON ACCOMPLISHMENTS AND GETTING STUFF DONE?

Stephen Covey, the iconic author and motivational thinker, told us to get into the habit of focusing on the "urgent" and "important" stuff.[1] David Allen, the self-help guru and bestselling author, gave us a foolproof system to "get stuff done," including a disciplined and highly effective way to declutter our growing piles of stuff.[2] And most recently, bestselling author Greg McKeown reminded us to focus on the "essential" stuff by following the "disciplined pursuit of less."[3]

> Managers stuck in the dilemma obsess about getting "stuff" checked off of their lists, but you will never go beyond the dilemma one check mark at a time.

These three ideas and their related tools are great, as are the countless other prescriptions that show us how to look at, sort, prioritize, and complete all of the stuff that our working lives demand. However, at the end of the day, it's all just "stuff." And because accomplishments are often just "one, and done" there is never enough TERF to get ahead. Think about the math for a minute: each fulfilled accomplishment only removes one item from your to-do list; however, each condition you create establishes the potential for multiple accomplishments to be realized. Rather than constantly falling behind in the dilemma's cycle of inefficiencies, this is how you *flip the scale* and produce positive, exponential value.

WHAT EXACTLY IS A CONDITION?

Reflect on your past few weeks at work, and name a positive outcome that you or your team achieved. Now, consider what had to be present in order for that accomplishment to happen. These enabling circumstances were your conditions. You can also flip the question and consider an example of a setback or disappointment that you experienced. Similarly, there were conditions present that increased the likelihood of the undesirable result taking place.

Technically speaking, I define conditions as the *patterns of interaction that facilitate a particular experience or outcome*. For example, when two colleagues work together over a period of time, they establish habits in the way they communicate and interact; the quality and experience of these habits create a condition.

To visualize this, imagine that our two colleagues enjoy a sense of positive regard toward one another, believe the other is sincere, and habitually offer their candid opinions and insights to each other in a free-flowing manner. With these interactions you might say they have a *condition of trust*, which is conducive to effective teamwork and collaboration. Hypothetically, if you were managing these two individuals and had to direct them to implement new procedures required by some mandated change, then you can easily imagine how this preexisting condition of trust would serve as an enabler to quickly and successfully make the required changes.

Alternatively, if these two colleagues do not hold each other in high esteem, if they do not believe the other is credible or sincere, and if they do not regularly communicate in transparent ways, then you can anticipate the kind of challenges you will face managing their attempts to implement the required change amid this underlying *condition of distrust.* Rather than the preferred pattern of trust that promotes collaboration and change, this pattern and its related conditions naturally limit the potential for effective teamwork and collaboration.

The critical insight here is that conditions never rest on a plateau; they are built up or eroded one interaction at a time. As anyone in a trustworthy working relationship knows, one breach of that trust can undo years of positive, respectful experience. And likewise, one trustworthy episode in an otherwise distrustful relationship can set a new course for something better.

Once they are formed, conditions are value-neutral until we assign judgment to them. Generally speaking, we label them as "preferred" when they produce the kinds of experiences and outcomes we want, or we call them "unwanted" when they block us. Unwanted conditions go by many names and descriptions. They are unhealthy, unproductive, limiting, destructive, confusing, and out of sync with priorities and goals. Preferred conditions also go by many labels. They are useful, productive, healthy, energizing, and aligned. They reflect back what is important to us, and although they may take time to cultivate, they are worth the effort because they allow us to both contribute and receive something valued. Conversely, unwanted conditions drain our motivation and TERF. They are just plain difficult, and ultimately they prevent us from both contributing and achieving the things we value.

Sometimes a condition develops quickly, while other times it evolves slowly over a longer period of time. Either way, conditions can be made and remade through the ongoing patterns of interaction we engage in with others. These are the everyday exchanges where decisions get made, relationships are built, team culture is solidified, and the trajectory for ultimate business outcomes get set into motion.

WHAT CONDITIONS ARE REQUIRED TO GO BEYOND THE MANAGER'S DILEMMA?

Conditions are unique to you, and it is your job to determine the balanced mix that will produce an environment that is conducive to your

needs. Based on the dilemma's specific obstacles, some of the most useful conditions that I coach managers to create include:

- Readiness—The preparedness to act at the right time
- Flexibility—The capacity to adapt to continuous change
- Insightfulness—The ability to discover meaning within complexity
- Diversity—The discipline of including divergent ideas and
  approaches
- Innovation—The willingness to let go of past success
- Development—The commitment to continuous learning and
  growth

Whatever conditions you choose to construct, it pays to remember
the advice from the influential Roman architect Vitruvius, who said any
good building should satisfy the three principles of *firmitas, utilitas*, and
venustas. Translation: as we create conditions for our teams to succeed,
they should be durable (the preferred condition will last), useful (the
preferred condition will produce desired outcomes), and beautiful (the
preferred condition will improve the quality of your experience).

HOW CAN I CREATE MY CONDITIONS?

What comes first? This powerful question is the key to creating your conditions. You need to answer that question and then set a reverse trajectory back from the experience or accomplishment you want. Following
this path leads you right back to the smallest building blocks that shape
your everyday interactions.

Turns are the step-by-step communication exchanges we have with
other people. When you say or do something before, during, or after an
interaction, it is a turn. Turns can be *fragmented* or *aligned* with our values and goals. With turns, there is typically an "action…reaction" pattern so what happened in the prior turn often influences what happens
next (e.g., you said this, so I said that, you did this, so I did that, etc.).

When you exchange a few turns with a noticeable start/end point,
you can give it a name and call it an episode. **Episodes** can be *open* or

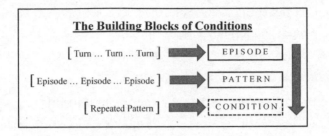

Figure 7.2   The building blocks of conditions.

closed toward the experiences and outcomes you want. For example, you may have experienced episodes such as "the difficult conversation," "the failed delegation," or the "excellent performance appraisal." If you string a few related episodes together that can be described with by a common theme, then you have a pattern.

Patterns of interaction become our conditions, and they can either be *preferred* or *unwanted*. Figure 7.2 shows what these interaction analytics look like, going from the basic turns we take from conversation to conversation, and how they accumulate in the episodes and patterns that shape our overall experience.

The quality of our working lives is a reflection of our conditions; so, if you want to transform something unwanted into something preferred, you have to get down to the level of turn in order to shift the episode's trajectory and ultimately make a new pattern. Look at these two examples and notice how the basic interactions (turns) initiated by these managers leads to episodes and patterns over time:

> When something goes wrong, I quickly step up and admit the mistake in order to be transparent about our real challenges. When I do this repeatedly, it leads to episodes of "honest communication and respect" and my team follows my lead and does the same. Over time, these episodes lead to patterns of "trustworthy behavior," which creates a condition of *high-performance collaboration.*
>
> I make sure that our team takes time to reflect on disappointments and failures without excessive blame. When we do this with the spirit of learning it leads to episodes of "problem solving and growth." As we

accumulate the positive lessons learned, we speak more candidly and disagree more comfortably on difficult issues. These episodes lead to patterns of "creative dissent," which generate a condition of *continuous innovation*.

HOW MUCH INFLUENCE DO WE REALLY HAVE ON CONDITIONS?

Whether we realize it or not, we are the strongest influence on the conditions that shape our everyday experience (we just do it without focused attention). Whenever we communicate and interact with other people, we place a building block in the structure of a condition. When you bring focused attention to what you "make" in each interaction, you learn how to shape your basic conditions. If we approach the interaction with little regard, then we leave the progress of that condition to chance.

Conversely, if we carefully communicate in ways that produce the experience we want, then we intentionally give the condition form. Once we realize the potential that conditions have to open up the possibilities we want, we can use them to our advantage. Since they typically involve other people, the unpredictability of human interaction means that we cannot control them. However, knowing the concrete ways in which conditions are made is enough to use your influence to shape them.

The Dilemma Up Close: Tom, an experienced manager, was handpicked by the chief innovation officer (CIO) to form an exploratory team. Their mandate was to figure out how to "get in front of major industry disruptions" that would likely pose a serious challenge to the organization. After tapping eight internal collaborators, Tom took immediate steps to meet the CIO's expectations—he scheduled a series of meetings to bring the group together and figure out what they could do before the shockwaves hit. However, after several failed efforts to get things moving, he still struggled to establish traction with the team. After three months of frustration, Tom invited me to help him get things on track.

"Our meetings aren't working!" Tom exclaimed during our initial discovery meeting. I wanted to understand this definitive statement and find

out what was really happening; so to edge into it, I simply asked him: What have you been doing for your meetings? In response, I heard a litany of tweaks and adjustments intended to correct a revolving set of unwanted outcomes. In Tom's own words:

We started out with a one-hour, biweekly meeting. I did not want to impose a heavy meeting schedule so I set up something 'short and sweet' for our touch points. After a month, it was clearly not working. There were a variety of gaffes and communication snafus that could easily have been avoided with more consistent face time.

So, I made the meetings longer in order to spend ample time exposing these gaps. With shifting priorities, it was essential to stay aligned so I told everybody we would take whatever time was necessary to get it right. But that didn't work either and the meetings just seemed to drag on. After another month, there was a growing sense that we were bogged down and wasting time. Recognizing the tension, I decided to change them from face-to-face to virtual.

My belief was that people could more easily get their work done, handle their customer responsibilities, and participate productively without the extra time burden of coming to the office for the two hours. I expected that a shorter, online collaboration format would leverage technology and create a better experience. But after another long month, it was clear that the online approach wasn't working like I hoped. Besides the frustration with occasional technology breakdowns, the communication was still ineffective. As a new group, we needed clarity around goals, roles, and priorities, but we were unable to establish them.

So, in the end, I went back to a shorter version of the face-to-face meetings. I made efforts to enhance them (i.e., rotating the facilitator, using multimedia tools, etc.), which brings us right back to the present where our meetings still aren't working!

For Tom, no matter how much he tweaked the superficial elements of the meetings, nothing changed the bottom line results. To help him see the reasons why the communication was blocked, I asked the question:

Setting aside the actual structure of the meeting, what would you say are the essential ingredients of candid communication and healthy discussion? His response was the opening to focus on the missing conditions required to achieve the teambuilding he needed:

I would say that it starts with participation; to offer something you have to be invested. Reflecting on this now, I realize that our group formed on paper, but we are a team in name only. Our prior roles remained relatively intact, which has made it easier for people to stick with their old routines. Besides the CIO's mandate, I've given them no reason to step up and invest in the possible innovations we have to explore.

Once we explored his ineffective meetings from this new perspective, the real challenge became clear. The "casual commitment" of the group influenced the tone of meetings so much more than the agenda or the format

---

Condition #1: *Readiness*

As a team we will do the little things that enable us to remain present, observant, and responsive to changing conditions. During meetings we will openly discuss issues and encourage alternative perspectives. We will stay with hard questions, not rush past them. And we will use our network to gain insights that extend our capacity.

The Blueprint ⟶

Turns – *In our everyday interactions we will challenge assumptions, take time to confirm our understanding, and be patient as each of us processes the change at our own speed.*

Episodes – *Building on these turns, we will use critical meetings to thoroughly explore multiple scenarios. We will not rush or get caught up by the pressure to charge ahead. We will move swiftly but deliberately.*

Patterns – *Those episodes will establish healthy habits of focus, clearer understanding of complexity, and honest assessment about implications of change. The patterns will make us <u>ready</u>.*

Figure 7.3 Creating the condition of readiness.

of their discussions. And if any substantive change was going to occur, he would have to shift from conditions of *complacency* to conditions of *full investment* and *readiness*.

Using the "condition of readiness" as a guide, we created a framework—beginning with the everyday turns—that would serve as a roadmap to establish the episodes and patterns necessary for his team's success (figure 7.3).

While every manager's job description requires them to initiate and lead lots of meetings, the true value they deliver is creating the conditions for the desired outcomes of meetings to be realized. In Tom's case, this condition of readiness was the missing piece he needed to activate the commitment and innovative spirit of his new team.

CHAPTER SUMMARY

THE EFFECT

When we focus exclusively at the end point of accomplishments, we miss our chance to influence the underlying factors that could increase our chances of success. Alternatively, when we focus on the underlying conditions where multiple experiences and outcomes are possible, we enable a more efficient use of our energy and potential. Learning how to engineer conditions is one of the most significant forms of organizational power you can develop.

THE HIDDEN INSIGHT

Although our conditions powerfully shape our experiences and outcomes at work, they lie just below the surface so we tend to focus more on the superficial tasks and achievements that we want. But it's not a question of "should I" or "shouldn't I"; we inevitably play a pivotal role in creating our conditions. We just do it without focused attention. The hectic pace of the manager's dilemma can make you think that things are random, but behind every experience and outcome there is always a set of specific conditions that made it possible and you were influential in creating them. Unfortunately, the dilemma delivers unwanted conditions that undermine our capacity to produce the outcomes that matter. To flip the scales, you have to be intentional about making your own.

THE RESPONSE

When the pace of change was less intense and our technology didn't keep us "on" 24/7, it was conceivable to spend a career shifting priorities and piles. Now managers need to accomplish multiple priorities simultaneously to make piles disappear. When we focus on the endpoints of our goals, by default we focus on one single path forward. However, when we focus on conditions, we open multiple paths to success. To create conditions, know your goal, then work backward by asking what has to come first? This reverse trajectory brings you back to the building blocks of conditions, which are the turns, episodes, and patterns of interaction.

THE SHIFT

The dilemma causes us to rush and react at the point of experience. The problem is that we have considerably less influence when things are happening in real time. To boost our influence over the experiences and outcomes we want, managers need to go upstream to the point of possibility. Meteorologists forecast the weather, but this is downstream stuff. The dynamic factors that actually influence the weather (i.e., climate) occur way upstream. Individual contributors can focus on weather, but managers have to think bigger and focus on climate.

Chapter 8

FIND THE POCKET OF INFLUENCE

Because there is only one *best chance* to get it right and that exists inside your pocket of influence

WHETHER IT IS A NEW PROGRAM YOU want to launch, a sensitive personnel decision you need to make, a bold new initiative you'd like others to support, or a controversial change that requires carefully coordinated execution, there are critical moments when the attitudes, motivation, and decision-making powers align to make things happen. I call these moments the *pocket of influence*.

Once we have created the required conditions for the outcomes we seek, these pockets are the optimal times to make our move and accomplish the priorities that matter to us. But what happens when the timing is not quite right or the elements you need in place are just not there?

Most of us have experienced the frustration that comes from an unsuccessful attempt to influence people and outcomes at work. These failures happen more frequently when we are stuck in the manager's dilemma because its burden reduces our capacity. When we are stretched thin, we often "swing for the fences" more out of desperation than as a well-timed choice to go big. Rather than maintaining focus

Figure 8.1   Find the pocket of influence.

on what's happening around us, we push ahead even when the risk of failure is high.

> In order to flip the scales and move beyond the grasp of the manager's dilemma, you need to leverage *minimal effort* for *maximum impact*.

However, if you can resist the temptation to steamroll ahead and instead find your pocket of influence, you can avoid these ill-timed, wasted efforts that dilute your impact. This more deliberate approach gives your solutions their full power and increases your chance of success.

This shift is important because within the constant triaging among valued and competing priorities, any failed effort to influence something important is equivalent to two failures. These produce the signature double-negative effect that the dilemma is so good at triggering. Not only did the change effort fail to produce the desired outcome, but we now have fewer resources to draw on for the next time. In some cases, there is the third-level effect as well, where residual damages from the original sideways attempt require additional time, attention, and damage control to repair.

In order to maximize your available resources and regain your full influence to have the impact you seek, you must find your pocket of influence. This chapter offers a *pocket guide* to help you extend your influence in the ways that matter to your success. Beginning with the characteristics of a good pocket, it shows you how to spot those critical moments of opportunity to make your move when the chances of success are greater than the risk of coming up short.

FEEL THE POCKET

In a moment of reflection, you can probably identify a critical time when you operated inside your pocket of influence. And vice versa, you can probably think of a time when you were decidedly outside of it as well. Focus on these two contrasting experiences to learn how to feel the pocket when it's present.

In the first scenario, you wanted to do or say something, and the perfect opportunity presented itself. The other person was receptive, you were on your "A-game" as you made a solid case, and things flowed perfectly. You got what you wanted, and it felt effortless. Remember what that felt like so you know how to sense a good pocket.

Now, think about the alternative experience where you wanted to say or do something yet you encountered immediate resistance. Maybe the other people involved were not in the right mood or mindset to listen, perhaps you were not in the best place to articulate a compelling case, or maybe you misread the situation and the actual thing you valued did not align with anyone else's priorities. Remember what that felt like too so you can anticipate the feeling when the pocket breaks down.

Regardless of the additional factors at play, in the latter scenario you got knocked out of your pocket and missed the opportunity to have the impact you wanted. In the first scenario, you operated from directly inside your pocket of influence and achieved the aim you set. These truly are the windows that open and close the access points to the outcomes we value.

Now that you understand the distinctions, consider the patience required to wait for your pocket to open, as well as the presence of mind to act wisely when you're caught outside of it. For example, would you walk into your boss's office first thing on Monday morning to ask for a raise? Would you bring up a controversial topic at a meeting that already ran over the stop time by 45 minutes and prevented people from getting to lunch? Would you risk your reputation by speaking out about a sensitive workplace issue that you did not think through or subtly test in advance with a few individuals?

> Although you cannot control your circumstances, a pocket helps you *time the moment* where your contribution can have the greatest influence on people and ideas.

On a good day, when your common sense is intact, you would not do these things. However, when caught up in the manager's dilemma, it can feel like there is no other choice but "now" because there is never enough time and therefore no such thing as a perfect moment. However, this is only a myth perpetuated by the dilemma's tactic to overwhelm and fluster us. Waiting for your pocket to develop may seem like a waste of time, but it is another way of *going slow to go fast*. To find your pocket, you must first understand its characteristics.

CHARACTERISTICS OF A POCKET

Think of the pocket of influence as a small buffer zone that allows you to momentarily pause and reflect long enough to utilize the full measure of your tools. This window enables you to assess the situation, clarify the objective, and use sound judgment about the best course of action to achieve it.

A pocket of influence is both a period of time and a condition where your intentional actions are more likely to affect the quality of the outcomes you get. Here are some of its characteristics:

- Although things happen lightning-quick, a solid pocket gives you a pivotal moment of pause where instincts and preparation can influence your decision-making.
- The pocket might initially be undefined, so you have to confidently step into the space as it develops in real time.
- Anytime you are knocked out of the pocket, you are subject to the dilemma's wide array of roadblocks—you may still succeed but not without the risk of a few false-starts.

The Dilemma Up Close: Jeff wanted a new kind of experience in his career, but he didn't want to leave the organization to find it. With no immediate promotional opportunities internally, he contemplated his options. After considering some of his ongoing frustrations about work, he got excited about an innovative approach that could overhaul this team's outdated sales process. He thought long and hard about the best way to take the idea to the managing director because he knew he would get only one chance to pitch the concept. Despite the potential risks of opening up the can of worms and having things go sideways, Jeff was ready for change and so he decided to roll the dice. But rather than just rushing forward, he took time to carefully consider the plan. He tested his ideas on a friend who could give him objective input, and he considered when the best time would be to make his move.

MAXIMIZE YOUR POCKET

Once it forms, to maximize your pocket of influence you have to be certain that a solid opportunity is present in the first place. In this context, opportunities are *desired circumstances where existing factors make it more likely that you will succeed in a given pursuit, rather than fail at it.* In other words, the odds are that we can make it happen, despite the fact that there are no guarantees. (When the chances of success and failure are equally unclear, the pursuit is more of a *risk* than a true *opportunity.*) To know whether the opportunity is there, think of it in four sequential stages to test the strength of it in the moment. Any solid opportunity is likely going to have these components:

1. *Recognition*—You and those you have to convince can clearly identify the issue as an opportunity (i.e., to change something, to start something, to stop something, to improve something, etc.). If you can see it, but they cannot, you do not have an opportunity yet. If there is a common language and mutual recognition, then test for the next element.

2. *Alignment*—Those you have to convince believe that you are the right person to champion the opportunity (i.e., you have the insight, you have the skill, you have the time, etc.). If there is no alignment, then the support you need for your ongoing involvement will not be there. If there is alignment and the "right people are on-board," then test for the next element.

3. *Timing*—You and those you have to convince believe that the time is now to pursue the opportunity (i.e., the urgency is there, the budget is not a problem, the window is open, etc.). If you can't confirm the timing, then you have an opportunity whose moment has not yet arrived. If the time is right, test for the final element.

4. *Execution*—You and those you have to convince trust that you can pull it off (i.e., you are prepared to overcome anticipated obstacles, the effort won't be wasted, etc.). If there is insufficient confidence in the capacity to execute, the window of opportunity will close. If it is present, however, then all four components are intact and the chances of success are high.

Opportunities are great and the pursuit of them can mark the pace of our career advancement and growth as professionals. When these factors are not present, you have a risk. The blind pursuit of uncertain risks—especially in the manager's dilemma—can derail you.

How many of us have tried in vain to push an opportunity through when the *recognition* or *alignment* was off? How many of us look back on failed efforts and blame other people or outside forces, rather than our own *ill-timed* choice to go forward? The next time you need to assess the strength of an opportunity, use these four elements to look for gaps. Looking at the anatomy of an opportunity isn't intended to stop you from doing what you want; it is just a guide to do what you want *when* you can achieve it the first time.

Once you validate the opportunity and feel the pocket of influence start to form, it is time to follow through. I will not provide scenarios or examples of how to maximize your pocket because they are too innumerable to list. Your specific role and the priorities you want to achieve are unique to you, so whether it is a new program you want to launch, a sensitive personnel decision you need to make, or a bold new initiative you want others to support, you just need to give your best effort to make it happen. As you do that, keep the following reminders top of mind to maximize your shot:

- *Don't talk yourself off of the ledge*; if the opportunity is solid and the pocket of influence is present, make the leap.
- *Don't rush for fear that the pocket will break down*; pockets eventually dissolve but trust that there is time to achieve what you want while it holds.
- *Don't listen to irrelevant voices of dissent*; you and those that have to be convinced matter, so limit your exposure to negative opinions outside that scope of influence.
- *Don't be afraid to try again if the pocket reopens*; sometimes the first effort provides the teachable moment for what has to change in order to get it right the next time.

TRIPPING POINTS

If timing is everything, the pocket of influence is the perfect time to make your move. However, the moment does not last and sometimes a pocket collapses quickly without warning. When there is a breakdown in the structure of the pocket, the temptation to scramble increases as the pace of action quickens. If the pain points from your manager's dilemma are acute, then the temptation to abandon ship is even greater. The following list reflects common tripping points to watch out for because they can knock us out of our pocket:

Getting disoriented—Sometimes the dilemma shifts the ground beneath us quickly, which leaves us disoriented and turned around. When that happens, reorienting yourself quickly is the best way to find an available pocket. To find yourself within your changing context, revisit your *line of sight* to mark your true North.

Eyes off the prize—When the dilemma puts us into a constant state of reaction, we stop looking ahead and lose focus on the horizon. In order to get your eyes back on the prize, bolster your *meaningful contribution* and be selective about the opportunities you pursue.

Forgetting you have a choice—When the dilemma makes us feel powerless, we believe that we do not have a choice in what happens around us. But that is a myth; we have greater influence than we think. Let this empowerment be the catalyst to *create the conditions* you need for a pocket of influence to surface when you need it most.

The Dilemma Up Close: Remember Jeff, the manager who was ready to pitch his new idea? Once he took time to carefully consider the plan and test his ideas, he waited for the pocket of influence to emerge. He noticed that the managing director followed a rhythm. The start of each week included a tightly packed set of meetings, but by midweek things seemed to open up. Jeff determined that this would be the best time to schedule the face-to-face. Anticipating the release of fresh financials the following Monday (which would undoubtedly cast the spotlight on the struggling sales team and bolster his pitch), Jeff picked that week to make his move. The pocket opened up beautifully: the managing director felt the pressure to boost the sales numbers, and this urgency made him receptive to an innovative approach. The preparation that Jeff completed prior to the meeting showed competence and passion for the project and within 30 days he had a new title and new career path.

CHAPTER SUMMARY

THE EFFECT

Because the dilemma spreads our capacity wafer thin, we have to make wise choices about how and when we use our limited TERF to make an impact. Inside the pocket of influence, the conditions and timing are right to influence people and create the outcomes we want. The pocket is not always a pivotal moment for major change. Sometimes it is just a small, incremental opening that can set us up something bigger. Regardless of its scope, it is *that moment* when you need to act.

THE HIDDEN INSIGHT

The constant strain from the manager's dilemma forms a monotonous cycle where everything looks and feels the same. However, there are critical moments—subtle openings of possibilities—all around. Sometimes we recognize and give names to these important turning points (i.e., my annual performance review where I will advocate for a promotion, the choice to confront a colleague about a growing concern, etc.) and at other times the moments surface and pass without our awareness of their potential to impact our working lives. If you can spot these moments, you gain leverage to use the pocket of influence to act.

THE RESPONSE

A solid pocket gives you a pivotal moment of pause where your instincts and preparation can influence your decision-making. Once you have verified the opportunity at hand (i.e., checking for recognition, alignment, timing, and execution), you have to take the leap and make your move. Although the pocket might initially be undefined, you still have to confidently step into the space as it develops. Anytime you are knocked out of the pocket, you are subject to the dilemma's wide array of road-blocks and obstacles.

THE SHIFT

Outside of the pocket, we tend to push and struggle to change immovable objects because the circumstances for fluid change are just not there. However, when we selectively step into a pocket of influence, our efforts and the potential for real impact are optimized. When we learn to recognize and act from within the pocket of influence, we flip the scales by leveraging *minimal effort* for *maximum impact*.

Chapter 9

CONVERT CHALLENGES TO FUEL

Because the dilemma will bury you in obstacles unless you *flip the scales* and find the path to performance hidden inside every barrier

IF OUR EVERYDAY HEADACHES AND challenges at work were a form of fuel, we would never run out of energy. As anyone who has spent even five minutes on the job can tell you, fuel is everywhere. However, for most of us these lingering obstacles are anything but small twigs and dry leaves that can be conveniently collected and used to start a productive fire. Instead, they take, take, and take from us in both direct and subtle ways.

From communication snafus to the challenges of unexpected change, the diverse setbacks we face exacerbate the effects of the manager's dilemma as they cause stress, undermine our motivation, and hinder our performance. Whether we make an effort to resolve them directly, or take time-wasting detours around them, they complicate our days and drain our TERF in inefficient ways.

Figure 9.1   Convert challenges to fuel.

Managers experience an assault of barriers from up, down, and across the organization. We're obligated to help our bosses eliminate their challenges. Our direct reports need our continual support to overcome theirs. And colleagues rely on us to help them resolve theirs too. As if this were not enough, we also face our own hidden challenges to working well.

More severe than the slow leaks discussed earlier, these issues can be referred to as gaps or obstacles, or they can be alluded to in more creative ways, such as *the things in the bushes*.[1] In general terms, labels such as hiccups, breakdowns, and blind spots all capture the general intent of the difficulty. I define them simply as *barriers to learning and performance*, and they show up incessantly in cubicles, offices, board rooms, break rooms, and out in the field, ready to keep you stuck in the manager's dilemma. Whatever form they come in and whatever name you give them, they are your fuel.

FUEL IS EVERYWHERE

To move beyond the dilemma, you have to go through your obstacles. I am not the first and I definitely will not be the last author to tell you there is a way to leverage your everyday adversity to accelerate your individual, team, and organizational performance. I admit, it sounds like alchemy: take something ordinary, if not unwanted, and turn it into something valuable. However, I actually did create a learning and development framework that is recognized around the world as an effective tool for transforming unwanted barriers to performance into clear and actionable change.[2]

The manager's dilemma loves to kill your momentum by throwing problems in your path to halt your progress. But what if you had a way to resolve those barriers at the time and place you encountered them? Rather than slamming the brakes, you could use this process to convert problems to fuel and accelerate through the dilemma's obstacle course.

This framework, which I have refined for nearly a decade now, enables you to identify a workplace challenge and shift its damaging effects to something better. It isn't magic and there are no short cuts or secret formulas. You need motivation to look differently at the issue and focused attention to work through it. The rest of this chapter will teach you how to convert your challenges to fuel, but before you jump in, consider a few of the common but undesirable responses we often have to our learning and performance barriers.

HEAD IN THE SAND
The *head in the sand* approach is an understandable, but highly ineffective, response that requires finding the largest rock available and

crawling under it. Along the fight, flight, or freeze continuum of reactions to trouble, this is the instinctive reaction associated with flight and freezing. When people feel disproportionately outmatched by their challenges, this avoidance response is often seen as the only recourse to outlast challenges that remain beyond their capacity. For managers waist-deep in the dilemma, this response sometimes feels like the only viable option.

BRUTE FORCE PROBLEM SOLVING

Brute force problem solving is admirable, but exhausting. This approach includes a combination of motivation to make things better *and* sheer frustration that the barriers showed up in the first place. The tactic here is to muscle your way through barriers and to try to outlast them with toughness. While some positive progress can be made, the majority of energy is usually spent resolving the presenting-level issues, so no systemic or lasting change occurs. There is often collateral damage as well as the people involved get bruised by this unsubtle approach.

THE CALVARY CALL

The Calvary call involves the use of a third party or outside resource to address the barrier. Whether it is a coach or consultant, the Calvary call occurs when you hear the loud swooping sound of an expert entering the picture for a short time to "fix the situation" and then exit just as quickly. Because of time limitations, the focus of their initiatives is often superficial. Therefore, things may improve in the short term, but the challenges inevitably resurface because the manager's dilemma remains intact, poised to regenerate the same barriers all over again.

Each of these typical reactions leaves us with *persistent deficit disorder*. Playing right into the dilemma's hands, our ineffective responses only deepen the impact of the barrier at hand and simultaneously drain our margin for meeting future challenges. But with a better response pattern, one that changes the paradigm, we can turn the tables for positive gain.

The Dilemma Up Close: Gil was the last to know about one of his escalating barriers. When Doug, his district manager, unexpectedly stopped by Gil's office, he anticipated a friendly chat. But what he got was a question with a bit of heat to go with it: *"Why are you late giving Sean his calculation tool? He was counting on you."*

A hard-working and accomplished manager, Gil was known for his straightforward approach to getting work done quickly and competently. Prior to Doug's inquiry, he thought things were going really well. His team was in good shape and he was even working with a leadership coach. But this turn of events took him out at the knees, and now he had to pivot and invest whatever energy it took to figure out what happened and how to resolve it.

Sean, another manager in the district, was only eight months into the job. From day one, he often sought out Gil for suggestions and best practices, which flowed freely during the first few months. The collegial relationship was solid, though lately Gil felt Sean should start relying less on him and take greater ownership for his portfolio of responsibilities. The calculation tool in question was an example of the unspoken, but troubled dynamic.

Two weeks earlier, Sean asked Gil to help him adapt the software tool for his use, but Gil didn't have time to do it. Unfortunately, rather than saying no respectfully and then taking time to explain his reasons, Gil made a weak commitment that sounded like "yes" to Sean but "no" to him. With hindsight, he recognized the trouble that his ambiguity caused. Gil felt frustrated that he was put in the situation to begin with: *Wasn't this Sean's problem in the first place?*

Despite his frustration, Gil wanted to make it right, and he was concerned that this barrier could undermine his standing with Doug. With a strong sense of urgency to avoid situations like this in the future, Gil converted the challenge into a source of fuel by making a Nav-Map. The process took him right into the heart of the issue and led to concrete action steps that he could take immediately to prevent it from happening again.

COLLECT YOUR FUEL

To convert your challenges into something useful, you need to collect your fuel. In most cases, your barriers are right in front of your nose; however, not every obstacle is worth converting. Some are structural issues that you couldn't change even if you wanted to, and still others may be in your influence but not in your *line of sight*.

Collecting the right kind of fuel starts when you scan your everyday experience on the job to locate both the presenting issues you face, as well as the deeper, root cause challenges that generate those barriers. If you don't have an obvious starting place, just think about a typical day at work and answer these questions:

What are your recurring headaches and challenges on the job? Maybe yours include some of these common barriers: there are communication breakdowns that diminish collaboration; there is too much change, so people become fatigued and indifferent; there are no clear roles, so people trip over each other with redundant efforts; or there is anxiety and distraction from information overload.

What are the deeper obstacles that put you in a state of frustration, stress, or crisis? Maybe yours include some of these more elusive barriers: the culture promotes competition, so teamwork suffers; people are afraid to speak up, so they don't share their perspectives freely; or people spin their wheels as they try to implement change without shifting the old attitudes and behaviors that keep the status quo in place.

Initially all you need to do is find a point of interest. You do not need a refined label or clear definition of exactly what the issue is right now because the process will take care of the rest. The most critical aspect with your fuel is just to find examples that you feel a sense of urgency and ownership with. Whether other people are involved doesn't matter either; you just need to recognize your stake in resolving it, as well as your plausible contributions to creating it in the first place.

The Dilemma Up Close: Courtney was an excited manager who had just volunteered to lead a special project for one of her company's Fortune 50 customers. This was the kind of opportunity she had been waiting for, and even though her plate was already full, she leapt at the chance to step up not knowing if the same prospect would come back again.

While her intention was good and the willingness to give more was admirable, the additional workload put Courtney into the *Danger Zone*, and as the little things started to slip, the effect of her manager's dilemma showed up during the first rocky interaction with the customer.

In a rush, Courtney sent over several lengthy documents about two hours before the initial meeting. Her intention was to reference them during the face-to-face discussion, then offer some suggestions about how they could further review and utilize them. She assumed that her counterpart would understand; however, his perception was quite different.

The email and its multiple attachments were viewed as a "request to read the documents" before the meeting and that created really strong push back. The meeting began with the client nearly shouting: *"Courtney, I don't know what you're used to, but here we show some courtesy. If you expected me to read that email for this meeting you should have given me more time!"*

This was not the kind of fuel that Courtney was looking for right out of the gate. She knew that it was always a bad idea to send things "cold" without a phone call to explain documents, but the dilemma caused her to rush without thinking. Her best practices went out the window in her scramble to keep up. Despite the misstep, Courtney decided to use the situation to her advantage. In this case the barrier was clear; she just needed to look inside it to pinpoint the missing element of performance.

After apologizing for the confusion, Courtney took the opportunity to negotiate clearer expectations for ongoing communication. Rather than assuming things about the level of detail the client wanted to be given, she offered a range of options. The discussion produced a healthy conversation and two concrete agreements that got the trajectory of the relationship on a better path. Had she been defensive or quick to rush past the initial challenge, Courtney would not have gotten the communication channel refined and she would have failed to show the client her responsiveness to the challenge.

In the bigger picture, this oversight was a wake-up call that helped Courtney see how much she was overextended and now at-risk of making other
errors. She used this inflection point to reflect on her priorities and delegate a few lesser obligations to free up additional TERF to manage her
new project effectively.

CONVERT CHALLENGES TO FUEL WITH NAV-MAPS

Unlike the dilemma itself, which is not a problem that can be solved, your
everyday headaches and challenges at work can often be quickly and
effectively resolved in ways that boost your learning and performance.
Your conversion tool is called a *Nav-Map* (short for navigation map),
and the remainder of this chapter will introduce you to this rapid conversion methodology, which has been used by leaders at every level with
great success. For managers caught in their own unique dilemma, the
four steps can be easily adjusted to fit a wide range of circumstances.

A completed Nav-Map provides a comprehensive snapshot of the
specific core barrier, multiple perspectives on the causes and conditions
of the issue, insight into the patterns that hold it in place, and the set of
committed actions required to transform it. The four related steps in
this progression require you to: (1) create a constellation; (2) test varying
perspectives; (3) find the trip-wire; and (4) set the action continuum.

With Nav-Maps, what was abstract becomes concrete as multiple
points of information and data are integrated into a set of four simple
diagrams. Because it is an infographic tool, the Nav-Map allows you
to rely on your visual capacity to understand a more comprehensive
picture of the problem *and* the solution to the barrier you select for
conversion.

The Dilemma Up Close: Remember Gil and the way his weak commitment
produced a collaboration barrier that got the unwanted attention of his
boss? A Nav-Map helped Gil clearly identify the factors that caused the

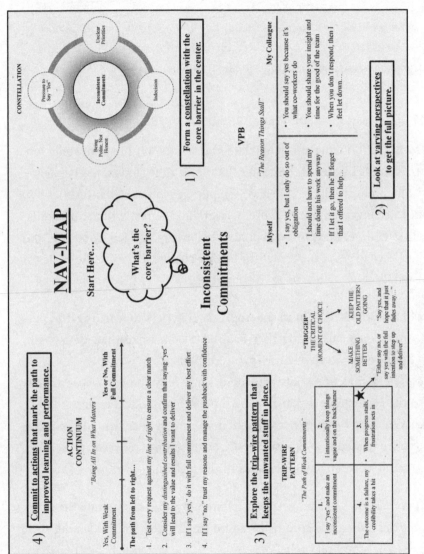

Figure 9.2 Nav-Map—inconsistent commitments.

breakdown and led to the unmet expectations with Sean and Doug. The good news for Gil was that his dilemma was still just hovering around the edges. It hadn't taken root in the heart of his working life, and so the process of converting his challenge into fuel solved the deeper issue and also served as a healthy reminder to *determine his line of sight* and *distinguish his contribution.* Both steps proved effective in preventing his dilemma from spreading further. Figure 9.2 illustrates his completed Nav-Map.

CONSTELLATIONS OF BARRIERS

A "constellation" is a pattern of related behaviors. Within a constellation, there is a core barrier at the center that holds other unwanted behaviors and outcomes in place. When you experience a constellation that you want to change, remove the core barrier and the rest will naturally dissipate over time. The physics that hold behaviors in place are strong, and so you have to get at the center for lasting change. Here are the basics of constellations:

- Like points of light in the night sky, barriers to learning and performance cluster together around a core issue that pushes and pulls other related barriers into relevance.
- The connections between them show how the core issue acts as the predictable link between all the other related barriers.
- When you experience a particular core barrier, you also experience related satellite barriers. Conversely, if you resolve the core, you resolve its satellite issues in the process.

If you attempt to change a constellation by addressing only the satellite barriers, then the core will remain unchanged and no lasting shift occurs. The temporary relief may help, but the systemic habits of behavior are left in place. Figure 9.3 illustrates the constellation from Gil's Nav-Map, which allowed him to objectively see his role in the situation and start untangling the mess.

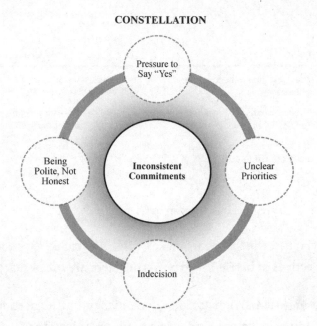

Figure 9.3   The constellation of barriers.

HOW TO CREATE A CONSTELLATION

1. Collect your fuel then select the most interesting example and ask: *"What is underneath this experience and what core issue holds it in place?"* Ask this question three successive times to drill deeper and discover the core.

2. Place the most prominent, root-cause barrier in the center of the constellation and explore additional questions such as: *What else does this barrier create* and *what seems to get pushed and pulled into your everyday experience because of it?*

3. Place these additional barriers in the peripheral circles and continue the process until the constellation is confirmed as accurate for the individual(s) involved.

VARYING PERSPECTIVES ON BARRIERS

Perspective shapes the way we understand ourselves and process our experience at work. Individuals have a hard time seeing beyond their

VPB

"The Reason Things Stall"

Myself	My Colleague
• I say yes, but I only do so out of obligation	• You should say yes because it's what co-workers do
• I should not have to spend my time doing his work anyway	• You should share your insight and time for the good of the team
• If I let it go, then he'll forget that I offered to help...	• When you don't respond, then I feel let down...

Figure 9.4   Varying perspectives on barriers.

own viewpoints, which is what makes VPBs—a visual snapshot of varying perspectives of barriers—so powerful. Here are the basics:

- Our view of barriers is fluid, dynamic, and influenced by factors like our role, tenure, and power in an organization.
- By seeing with one perspective, we naturally do not see from others—and each unique vantage point is in some way accurate, but never absolutely complete.
- By expanding our own perspective, we bring more information into our field of view and create a bigger picture.

The example from Gil's Nav-Map in figure 9.4 illustrates the varying perspectives on barriers that expanded his picture of exactly what happened and why. This step opened up new vantage points to understand and take ownership for his role in the situation. It also proved to be a cathartic experience that helped to reduce his frustration and see more clearly about what he wanted to do moving forward.

HOW TO CONTRAST VARYING PERSPECTIVES ON BARRIERS

1. Identify the people/perspectives most affected by the core barrier in the constellation and plot the people or perspectives across the "T-Bar." (Gil's example has two, but you can plot as many stakeholders or distinct perspectives as you need to.)

2. Consider how the issue is experienced, including the causes and conditions that sustain it, and write down representative bullet points. The simple prompt here is: "How do you see this issue playing out, and if you had to, what name would you give it?"

3. Once all VPBs are named, contrast them with questions like: "What's different about the way we see things? How do we see things the same? What happens when we single out just one of the perspectives and call it the 'right' one?"

TRIP WIRE PATTERNS

Sometimes the same barrier just keeps showing up in our experience. This happens when our reactions to specific situations "trigger" it into effect. Although the experience and outcomes are unwanted, we end up sustaining them through our own counterproductive choices and actions. I call these *unseen trip wires to change*. If our habits of interaction turn into these repeat reactions, then the way to shift them is to spot the critical moment of choice that can either sustain or alter the pattern. Here are the basics of trip wire patterns:

- The conditions that sustain our barriers are often furthered by our own subtle behaviors that obscure our role in the matter and distract us from the root cause of the issue.
- Drawing a trip wire pattern allows you to more objectively map the attitudes and behaviors related to the core barrier to see how they are sustained.
- To convert the barrier, you have to find the "trigger point" that activates the pattern, and then alter the conditions to disrupt the status quo.

The example from Gil's Nav-Map in figure 9.5 illustrates the trip wire pattern that finally exposed his pattern of weak commitments with Sean. This proved to be an important moment both of recognition and of ownership for making immediate change.

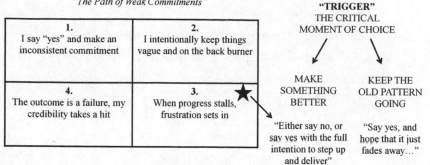

Figure 9.5   The trip wire pattern.

HOW TO IDENTIFY A TRIP WIRE PATTERN

1. Create the "trip wire" grid and identify the four basic elements that shape the pattern. Start with the first action then put each successive turn in "sequence" within the boxes (going clockwise from top-left).

2. Identify the critical moment of choice and put a star by it. Answer the question, *"What can I do differently to shift the pattern?"*

3. Contrast the two paths forward: the status quo will keep the trip wire pattern in place; the critical moment of choice will make something better.

ACTION CONTINUUM

You have to know where you are to know where you are going. The "action continuum" lets you plot your starting place in relation to the barrier you're dealing with, then set actions to move toward your goal of improved learning and performance. Here are the basics of an action continuum:

- The resolution of the barrier lies within the issue itself because the learning and performance element or goal is like a barrier in reverse.

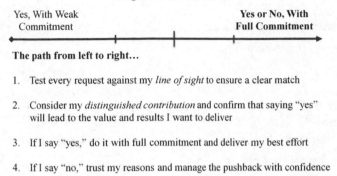

Figure 9.6 The action continuum.

- If you turn the barrier inside out and stretch it, you find a pathway to convert it.
- Drawing the continuum stirs the questions: *"Where am I right now?"* and *"What is required to begin moving from left to the right toward the goal?"*

Figure 9.6 displays the action continuum from Gil's Nav-Map. It shows a path toward stronger commitments, which eliminates the ambiguous, half-hearted choices he made before. Moving forward Gil wanted a "yes" to mean *yes* and a "no" to be something he could clearly and confidently articulate. This was all about developing decisiveness as a leader and maintaining the clarity in his commitments. Each new action step reflected a practical move in his desire to shift.

HOW TO CREATE AN ACTION CONTINUUM

1. Create a single line and place the core barrier from the constellation on the left side of the continuum, and then plot the desired change—the inverse learning and performance aspiration—on the far right side.
2. Consider your current location as of "right now," and then mark the spot on the continuum. (If there are multiple individuals or opinions about the starting point, take an average.)

3. Using the last picture as a guide (i.e., the "critical moment" to shift the trip wire pattern), identify two–four key actions that will move you from left to right. You do not have to change everything overnight; you just want a few carefully selected actions that can create incremental movement.

UNPACKING NAV-MAPS

Now that you have seen an example and reviewed the steps, here are a few closing thoughts about the versatility of Nav-Maps and some suggestions for using them.

TIME VERSUS BENEFIT

Gil took about 45 minutes to complete his Nav-Map. It took some time to initially review the steps, figure out how the four pictures worked together, and gain some confidence drawing it out. And there were definitely some trash can basketballs tossed when the first few iterations were abandoned. But once his constellation came together, things started to click, and he got the momentum he needed to follow through.

When you are stuck in the manager's dilemma, taking 45 minutes to address a situation might seem like too much time. But can you really afford not to make the effort and just let the problem linger?

Although his Nav-Map require a bit of work, as the influential philosopher Wendell Berry would say, it was designed to *solve for pattern*. Gil's insights and solutions could address multiple problems simultaneously, while reducing the creation of new collateral issues. This translated to getting his problem solved right the first time and leaving the baggage behind. Rather than avoiding barriers or responding in one of the three common, yet wholly ineffective ways I mentioned earlier, Gil's effort paid off because the issue got resolved and the way he took ownership for his part of the challenge likely strengthened the respect his boss had for him.

NAV-MAPS DELIVER COMPETITIVE ADVANTAGE

The introduction of this book made it clear that there are no shortcuts or easy answers to manage through the challenges of the dilemma.

Learning how to convert challenges to fuel is probably the most difficult tool to implement. However, leveraging your obstacles for growth isn't just an edge, it's *the* edge you need.

The tools you need to make Nav-Maps offer a predictive approach to identifying and resolving performance problems. When a manager develops the competency and discipline to do this for themselves and for others, they elevate their contribution to the developmental domain.

Not long ago, a good manager was defined as one who could take charge, call the shots, and operate in a traditionally hierarchical manner. "Don't tell me about the labor pains, just show me the baby!" Although this approach is still acceptable in some specialized environments, that is, law enforcement, emergency response, and so on, in business it has given way to the facilitative style of management.

This offered a progressive shift away from top-down authority to a greater focus on collaboration. In this transition, managers went from assuming *top-down authority* to trusting in their team's *collective ability* and inspired action. They went from *knowing what to do*, to knowing *how to use versatile tools* to get the job done. They pivoted from search for *the right decision* to seek the *power of the group's diversity* and the benefits of diverse perspectives. Also, they shifted from a reliance on their own *individual charisma and ability* to decisions that the team could own and implement through their *personal commitment*.[3]

As anyone who has worked for a leader with a severely hierarchical style can tell you, the difference between these two approaches is dramatic. However, there is a third shift under way that promises an even greater distinction between the facilitative approach and what I call *developmental management*.

In this approach, the facilitative tools are all still relevant for managers to leverage, but the relative shift tilts toward building capacity for each individual to exercise intelligent learning and performance. This deep commitment to continuous learning and performance occurs when managers implement self-reinforcing tools that enable individuals to independently reproduce cycles of learning that adapt with the changing environment and produce increasingly valued and relevant results for their teams.

Specifically, the mindset of a developmental manager is different when it comes to problems. Rather than headaches to avoid, they are fertile ground for learning. Delays are not frustrations, and detours are not necessarily bad or unwanted. The relentless focus on learning converts every unexpected or unwanted outcome into an opportunity to respond differently the next time. In other words, they use tools like Nav-Maps to delve deep into their frustrating obstacles to leverage the insight of learning that it holds for better performance next time. This is how managers create and deliver value and distinguish themselves among the rest.

OUR BARRIERS ARE DATA

When we are immersed in the manager's dilemma, its overwhelming effect causes us to stop looking anywhere but straight ahead. However, there is plenty to see if we take time to look. Our barriers are a source of vital data about what's working, what's not working, and why. Information that sheds light on our learning and performance is everywhere because we are enmeshed in constant feedback loops regarding our choices and behaviors that either move us toward our goals, or backfire and lead us astray. The problem is that most of this information is difficult to pinpoint and cumbersome to organize.

Nav-Maps help you decode difficult situations like the one Gil experienced, and they also produce actionable results. In the big picture, the two primary goals of Nav-Maps are to: (1) help you better understand and manage the current events and challenges brought on by the manager's dilemma; and to (2) use the data to better predict what will likely occur in future situations so that you can create the preferred conditions where those problems occur less frequently and with decreased impact.

FOLLOW SUBSTANCE OVER FORM

Keep in mind that Nav-Maps are my preferred way of working through the conversion process. However, if drawing constellations or any of the models feels too complicated, use the simplest combination of tools and approaches to most effectively create the change you want. This means that rather than trying to "do the process right," you simply do what is useful, no matter how far off script you need to go.

CHAPTER SUMMARY

THE EFFECT

Every manager—regardless of title or tenure in the organization—encounters a constant barrage of barriers to learning and performance that sustain the manager's dilemma. But these challenges are a form of fuel that can be converted into a vital resource. Effectively identifying and resolving these unavoidable challenges actually *flips the scales* on the dilemma; it's the key to accelerating your advantages as you edge back toward your *Performance Zone*.

THE HIDDEN INSIGHT

If we avoid or try to outrun or out-muscle our everyday headaches and challenges at work, they only wear us down and cause unproductive side-effects. We need a better response, one that explores them confidently and exploits their teachable moments for our own gain. Rather than accepting or avoiding them, we can interrogate and ultimately transform them: (1) What is the root cause of my challenge? (2) How can I see it from various perspectives to get the full picture? (3) What underlying behavior holds the unwanted experience and outcome in place? (4) What immediate action can I take to resolve the challenge? Responding to these questions allows you to draw an accurate Nav-Map, which offers a fluid transition from obstacle to opportunity.

THE RESPONSE

Nav-Maps are visual pictures that organize the hidden causes and drivers of barriers. In a few minutes, you can use the tool to complete the conversion process by identifying the underlying issues, different perspectives, and behaviors that keep the challenge in place. The final step is a series of committed actions that transform the pitfall into a pathway for a better outcome and experience.

THE SHIFT

It's only when things are challenging that we can gain a true measure of who we are and what we're capable of doing. When we run toward our barriers, rather than away from them, we learn the important discipline of *being comfortable outside of our comfort zone*. This increases our confidence and capacity to respond to the dilemma when it invariably knocks us out of our sweet spot. And when it does, rather than enduring barriers that drain your TERF, you can turn them into fuel and *flip the scales* of the dilemma by accelerating your impact.

Chapter 10

MAKE YOUR GOALS THEIR PRIORITIES

Because in the space between what matters to you and what your team and organization need, there is a mutual agenda that keeps you first

THE MANAGER'S DILEMMA THREATENS us with scarcity. The unending cycle of "never enough" time, energy, resources, or focus to meet the increasing demands we face can produce a destructive competition between individuals and organizations, with managers stuck in the middle.

The threat shows up in both obvious ways and in more subversive patterns. The friction is palpable when priorities, mandates, and desires conflict and self-interest rises above shared concerns. Here are several ways it shows up, beginning first at the individual level.

At an individual level—regardless of title or role—we all experience the conflict within our own set of responsibilities. The push and pull of irreconcilable choices when you cannot get it all done causes the split: *Which priority do I focus on above all the others? Which request do I respond to even though they are all important?* These are examples of the critical assessments, judgment calls, and decisions that frame the

Figure 10.1 Make your goals their priorities.

zero-sum game we play when there is never enough. The result is an undermining competition with ourselves!

Within our relationship with the organization, the conflict is framed by the indisputable death of the *psychological contract*. This phenomenon, held in place for generations, was a silent pledge understood clearly by both employees and organizations. It meant that if employees dedicated their careers in loyal service to the company, the company would in turn reward them with lifelong employment and a pension. Fractured long ago, this trade for stability in exchange for service was replaced by the era of "the free agent employee"[1] and "the cost-cutting organization."

On the employee side, individuals struggle to capitalize on personal opportunities amid the volatility and change of the economy, while knowing full well that their jobs could be downsized, outsourced, or

automated any time without notice. On the organization side, companies stand ready and willing to restructure the workforce, and indeed
the entire operation, when the prior quarter's sagging profit margin
requires it or shareholders demand it.

> Managers are like referees. They work for the league (organization), but
> they're also supposed to impartially represent the interest of the players
> in the game (employees). When they make the right call, they get no
> special thanks because—after all—it's their job. But when they make a
> mistake, they get unfair accusations from every direction. It is thankless
> work sometimes, but the game could not go on without it.

The degree to which employees, managers, and organizations resolve
these distinct, but related threats sets the trajectory for not only the
company's bottom line performance, but also for the culture and quality of working life that everyone experiences. But as long as the threat
of mutual competition is viewed as an inescapable either/or choice, the
future is bleak because there can only be winners and losers.

To flip the scales and finally go beyond the dilemma's pull, this chapter offers a plan for crafting a strong *mutual agenda*. At the heart of the
concept is the belief that in order to get more of what you want, you have
to give people what they need. Call it a golden rule that the manager's
dilemma cannot break; it is the way to make your goals a welcome and
essential part of others' priorities.

> As a manager, your job is to give, give, and give. You give your time, tal-
> ent, and attention to your direct reports to help them succeed in their
> roles and meet the team's objectives. You give your time, talent, and at-
> tention to senior leaders to support their strategic goals and ensure mis-
> sion and financial success. Collectively, all of your resources flow into the
> organization in these direct and subtle ways, but when does the invest-
> ment come back to you?

How can you inspire others when you're uninspired? How can you give clear direction when you're going in circles? How can you make great decisions when your own priorities are elusive? Going beyond the manager's dilemma restores your full capacity to give these things, but *your* success depends on what you get back.

To succeed over the long haul, you have to learn how to advocate for and accept the commensurate support you offer to others. Whether you manage 1 or 100 other people, there is a *mutual agenda* where your own aspirations for your career and the quality of working life you seek will align with the specific needs of your team members and the larger organization. Creating yours will allow you to convert the scarcity and competition it brings into focused alignment and cooperation.

UNDERSTANDING THE MUTUAL AGENDA

The fact is that individuals and organizations are stuck with each other. You cannot have organizations without employees, and successful employees align their contributions to fulfill the intended purpose of the company. Brokering this delicate middle ground, managers play a pivotal role in facilitating the success of both. To produce reciprocal gains, you have to establish and maintain a clear and compelling mutual agenda, which is the powerful space *where individual goals intersect with team priorities and organizational objectives.*

Despite their leadership role, managers are not exempt from conflict. As organizations compete for talent without long-term commitment, and individuals compete for work and wages with the greatest degree of upward mobility, managers must negotiate this perilous balancing act with their employees *and* for themselves as their own careers progress.

Similar to line of sight, a mutual agenda is an overlapping set of priorities that coordinates alignment between important objectives among stakeholders. When fully present, a strong mutual agenda resolves the threats described earlier and replaces them with a virtuous cycle of engaged performance.

BENEFITS OF THE MUTUAL AGENDA

If you take off your management hat for a second and think about your-self as an individual contributor (and we all are at some level), oper-ating within the mutual agenda activates your focus, motivation, and positive outlook toward work in the short term. In the long term, your value-added contributions will improve your overall performance and open access to choice assignments and increased opportunities for advancement.

When you consider yourself in the role of a manager, responsible for executing strategy and driving organizational success, understand-ing the strategic importance of the mutual agenda and cultivating its boundaries is about engagement and retention in the short term. In the long term, it improves bottom-line performance as the culture becomes shaped by engaged people, contributing their best effort, doing excellent work, and attracting others who will do the same.

As a manager, your role requires you to help others perform at their best. It is not necessary to assume an altruistic viewpoint to recognize that enabling the strong and consistent performance of your team offers a direct reflection of your own success leading them. Show me a man-ager whose direct reports fail consistently over time, and I'll show you a vacant manager's role!

> *A leader's purpose is to help others discover their own.* However, you can't do this when you're stuck in the manager's dilemma. Flipping the scales enables you to regain your capacity to stay actively engaged as the vital touch point they need to define and pursue their path to success.

If you ask 100 employees how they would define a "good manager," they would likely describe characteristics like these: present, attentive, supportive, etc. This is because *good managers are the scaffolding for others to climb.* In fact, one of the largest human resources studies of its kind showed that:

> Employees who are satisfied with their manager state a much higher intention to stay with the organization than those who are dissatisfied. Those who rate their managers as good also feel they have promising prospects within the company as well as confidence in the organization's future. [And] those employees who regard themselves as working for a good manager have three-four times higher engagement scores than those who work for managers they regard as ineffective.[2]

Conversely, according to the Corporate Executive Board, when employees work for a "bad manager," their level of performance can suffer for up to five years as a result of the residual, negative effects from the experience.[3] Considering this, it is clear that there is a strong economic incentive for managers to fully invest in their people by crafting a mutual agenda. Beyond the dollars and cents, however, the positive contributions we make to others can create cultures of collaboration where boomerang employees and alumni often come back to help us in surprising ways.

The following two-part framework is a guide for managers to establish a strong mutual agenda. In the first part, the focus is on concrete ways that managers can establish expectations and support, which deliver a foundation for their teams to contribute at their best. Part two returns to the theme of "paying yourself first," and it offers a straightforward set of recommendations on how to ask for and accept support up, down, and across your place on the organization chart.

FRAMING THE MUTUAL AGENDA: PART ONE—SUPPORTING OTHERS

Do you know what each of your team member's personal goals are? If you do not have a clear sense of what matters to them and where they would like to go, rest assured that you will eventually find out. Unfortunately, it will likely be in the form of an ultimatum or resignation letter. The clear message is: *get comfortable asking questions about how your people are really doing, what's working and not working, and what people need to feel like their work is aligned with their own values and goals.*

Follow me through this thought exercise for a moment. First, put yourself in the shoes of a team member for a moment. Now, imagine your manager schedules uninterrupted time for a face-to-face meeting and asks you the following three questions, and then legitimately offers the related commitment of support.

1. Where do you want to go? *Let me help you get there.*
2. What do you need to accomplish to get there? *Let me help you make it happen.*
3. What stands in your way? *Let me help you overcome it.*

First, how would you answer these questions? And second, what would you think about a manager who took the time to understand your responses and then stepped up to deliver credible support to realize them? If we call the answers to these questions our "reasons," then the first step to crafting a mutual agenda for people is *to understand their reasons* and invest in fulfilling them. Once you do that, the trajectory is set and things become much more straightforward.

The next step in crafting a structurally sound mutual agenda for your direct reports is to provide a mix of both *expectations* and *support*. When it comes to expectations, managers should set forth clear requests that not only support team goals, but also elevate the employee's impact on the organization (think line of sight). This makes the individual contributor look good and it supports the important objectives of the company. To do this, there are a few key actions managers can take:

1. *From day one, create expectations early and reinforce them often.* This includes role clarification, goal setting discussions, and specific (written) lists of shared responsibilities;
2. *With the trajectory set, stay present enough to track their ongoing efforts and progress in meaningful ways.* This requires one-on-one

meetings (weekly/biweekly), time spent observing and providing instant feedback, and open channels of communication to address inconsistencies between expectations and performance.

3. *Communicate early and often when accountabilities are unmet.* This looks like both formal and informal feedback discussions focused on concrete examples, behaviors, and outcomes that balance a mix of both support and responsibility for the individual.

Factors like these can create half of a strong mutual agenda where both employees and organizations increase their odds of success. Without it, high potential employees will feel underchallenged and may leave to find better opportunities. And borderline or struggling employees may continue to fly under the radar. With clearer expectations in place, managers can also then elevate the level of support they give to their people to help them grow at an accelerated pace.

Table 10.1 illustrates the natural overlap between an individual's priorities and the larger organization's goals. In this case, the employee felt like he had no choice but to leave the company in order to meet his career goals. Ironically, the organizational objectives (published on the company's own official website) promised a direct match. Although expressed differently, look at the fit between the individual's priorities and the organization's strategic goals.

Table 10.1   Overlapping priorities frame the mutual agenda

Individual's priority (to outperform my place on the org. chart)	*Organization's goal* (to attract and retain top talent)
• I want to learn, grow, and advance	• We need contributors to adapt and evolve
• I want to tackle big problems	• We need change-minded innovators
• I want to feel motivated and passionate	• We need people to go above and beyond
• I want to be challenged to lead	• We need to grow future leaders

Turnover is an equal opportunity pain point, and so it helps everyone to reduce it when possible. In this case, common ground was achieved before the solid performer walked out the door (thanks to the quick thinking of the manager who played the "connect the dots" role and helped the person gain confidence in future opportunities).

In your own team, use this example as a guide to consider how the desires of your people may directly support the team and organizational goals that matter. How could both be achieved simultaneously, without unnecessary competition? And if there is no justifiable alignment, then how can the mismatch be dealt with in a manner most expedient and advantageous to all parties?

TEST YOUR SUPPORT

Despite the collapse of the psychological contract between individuals and organizations, managers can step into that void and deliver something useful to both parties. This new contract starts when managers make a personal investment in their people, and people do the same in return. For individuals, the expectations and support described earlier are often the missing link required to frame their mutual agenda.

If you want to know how you are doing, then you can test how they perceive your support. Imagine we did a little workplace anthropology and interviewed some of your team members to measure how effectively you show up for them. Or better yet, imagine you gave the following eight-question survey in table 10.2 to your key reports. What would they say about the investment you make in them?

Inviting your people to answer questions like these can help you assess your effectiveness at delivering the value that fills in a critical aspect of their mutual agenda. Once you step up and deliver, you cannot work harder than they do; the rest is up to them.

FRAMING THE MUTUAL AGENDA: PART TWO—INVESTING IN YOURSELF

Once you consistently take care of your people and deliver your end of the bargain for their mutual agenda, it's time to pay yourself. For a

Table 10.2 How does my manager invest in me?

Question	Ranking
1. My manager is present, engaged, and accessible	Always, Sometimes, Never
2. My manager helps me see my role and contribution in relation to the big picture	Always, Sometimes, Never
3. My manager makes it easier for me to get great work done	Always, Sometimes, Never
4. My manager contributes to my growth and development	Always, Sometimes, Never
5. My manager provides direction about priorities	Always, Sometimes, Never
6. My manager empowers me to say "no" to distractions	Always, Sometimes, Never
7. My manager understands the true demands of my job	Always, Sometimes, Never
8. My manager does the little things (i.e., listening, following-through, giving feedback, sharing credit, etc.) that make a big difference in my performance	Always, Sometimes, Never

manager to successfully craft her mutual agenda, she needs to know what she wants to contribute, what she wants to achieve, and how these factors link with the career experiences and opportunities she values (the preceding chapters offered a variety of tools to clarify some of these important details).

Once these things are clarified, she is better positioned to advocate for circumstances that are conducive to her success, such as access to better assignments and increasing responsibilities that align with core values and aspirations. It is possible to give up, down, and across the organization without losing sight of your own needs. The key is to build in your own model of reciprocity along the way. To illustrate practical

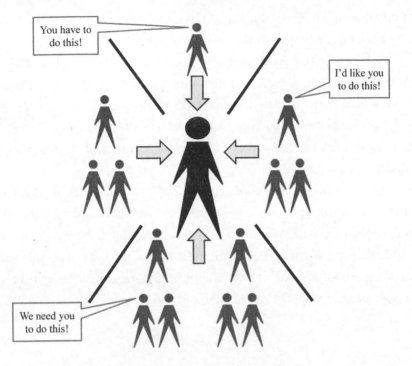

Figure 10.2 Managers contribute in three dimensions.

ways of drawing on all of these layers of support, consider the three dimensions in which mangers operate (figure 10.2).

As you consider the key individuals that impact your experience at work, scan up, down, and across your sphere of influence. Who are these people, what are their names, what do they ask of you—and now more importantly—what can you ask of them?

ACROSS—Be a champion for your colleagues to succeed, and ask for their support with your important projects; invite them to share honest feedback in areas you want to grow; seek their involvement as advocates of priorities you care about; and use them as a sounding board to respond wisely to the challenges and opportunities you encounter.

UP—Be a catalyst for senior leaders to achieve their strategic goals, and ask for their time in return; invite them to share feedback and leadership lessons; give them reasons to want to sponsor your development and then make the request; and finally learn how to negotiate with them so that when you need to say "no," it is understood in a way that doesn't limit your future opportunities.

DOWN—Be the scaffolding for your people to climb, and delegate effectively so that they carry the load for the team; hold them accountable so that their performance reflects well on your management; and rely on them for ideas and support so that the brunt of challenges facing the team is distributed across the range of talent and commitment in the group.

In each of these three domains, the foundational theme is "don't act alone." As a manager, you have to own the mandate and take the first steps to go beyond your dilemma. However, you must rally support along the way. Without it, your personal half of the mutual agenda goes missing. And if you do not establish the boundaries to ask for and accept the elements of support you need to fulfill your goals, then who will?

CHAPTER SUMMARY

THE EFFECT

The manager's dilemma provokes a threatening sense of scarcity because there is just never enough time, energy, resources, or focus to get it all done. This can result in a destructive competition between individuals and organizations, with managers stuck in the middle. A solution to this vicious cycle is discovering the *mutual agenda* where individual goals and both team and organizational needs intersect. Managers can help their direct reports establish their agenda, but they also have to "pay themselves first" and create their own.

THE HIDDEN INSIGHT

Creating your *mutual agenda* allows you to flip the scales on the dilemma by converting competition for resources into focused alignment and cooperation. The mutual agenda shows that it is possible to get a two-for-one that reduces the tension from these "scarcity threats" and twists the adversarial mindset into something more cooperative. Finding out how the specific things you value and need correspond to what others require produces a win-win scenario.

THE RESPONSE

To help others create their mutual agenda, managers can ask questions to understand the personal goals of their team members, and then offer a balance of both expectations and support, including: Where do you want to go? *Let me help you get there.* What do you need to accomplish to get there? *Let me help you make it happen.* What stands in your way? *Let me help you overcome it.* This is the necessary mix that enables employees to maximize their investment of time in an organization by defining and pursuing their own long-term career goals while staying true to their team and organization's needs.

Likewise, managers can maximize their mutual agenda by clearly and consistently advocating for and accepting the support they need up, down, and across their place on the organization chart. From peers, seek their involvement as advocates of the priorities you care about. From bosses, invite them to share feedback and their lessons learned and give them reasons to want to sponsor your development. And from direct reports, rely on them for ideas and support so that the brunt of challenges facing your team is distributed across the range of talent and commitment in the group.

THE SHIFT

It is in this middle ground of a mutual agenda where breakthrough performance can happen, but it can only be discovered through honest conversations about what matters most. When there is alignment and a clearly accepted mutual agenda, momentum from the synergy serves as a counterbalance to complacency and performance gaps that often surface when employees and organizations inadvertently work against each other.

CONCLUSIONS

An inevitable, self-sustaining bind suppresses your capacity to perform at your best when the inverse equation of shrinking resources and increasing demands takes hold in your working life.

THIS IS THE MANAGER'S DILEMMA

It's the easy improvement you don't have time to make.
It's the good advice you don't have the energy to follow.
It's the logical next step you're too resource-strapped to take.
It's the obvious solution you're too distracted to notice.

To avoid these dangerous traps, put this book's ideas into practice Monday morning and share them with your team—because the best way to learn something new is to teach someone else.

WHEN I THOUGHT ABOUT THE BEST WAY to conclude *The Manager's Dilemma*, I considered closing things out with a bit of truth telling that would powerfully sum up my key messages:

The manager's dilemma is here to stay. When business is good, the dilemma spikes because the growth curve pushes everyone's capacity to the edge. When business is bad, the dilemma spikes because the belt tightening pushes everyone's capacity to the edge, just for the opposite reasons. The cycles of the dilemma will come and go, but if you overcome it once, you can beat it again, and that gives you the upper hand.

From your first promotion to manager, you unequivocally joined the leadership group of your organization. The argument about whether managers are leaders is a false premise; everyone must lead at whatever level they're at. To lead well you need to maximize your capacity, leverage your talent, and take advantage of your opportunities. The best way to reach your full potential is to go beyond the constraints of the manager's dilemma.

Optimism isn't enough to escape the grasp of the manager's dilemma; you also need a plan. There's an anonymous poem that reflects inspired optimism, but shows just how empty it is without an escape hatch: "The optimist fell ten stories, and at each window bar he shouted to the folks inside: 'Doing all right so far!'" The eight strategies presented in this book offer both a silver lining and a proven strategy to stop the free fall.

After reflecting on these statements, I realized that they were important, but there was something else more fundamental that I wanted to offer as parting words. So, I chose to end the book with this call to action:

If you do nothing else, teach these ideas and share these tools with your teams. The eight core strategies presented in The Manager's Dilemma *are absolutely crucial for managers stuck in the dilemma, but they're also relevant to individual contributors who also feel overworked and overwhelmed. Many of the same drivers that fuel and sustain the inverse equation are present for your people; hence, investing in their capabilities to overcome them is actually an investment in yourself.*

To unpack the last piece of this closing thought—*an investment in your team is an investment in yourself*—think about your toughest experiences as a manager. The examples that come to mind probably include times when you have had to address tricky performance issues with struggling team members. These dynamics are another form of weight, and they not only burden you, but one failing contributor forms a drag on the rest of your team's capacity to operate effectively.

If it was just one thing, then we would overcome it, make the change, and achieve the desired result. But the manager's dilemma is not just one thing; it's the accumulation of compounding challenges that trap us in counterproductive patterns that drive us past the breaking point. How will your impact grow when you invest time to help others reverse these challenging effects and restore their full capacity to go from breakpoints to breakthroughs?

To alleviate the burden of declining performance, help individuals succeed, and give your entire team what it needs to flourish, create a win-win-win by teaching others to move beyond their dilemma. The final pages include eight short teaching tools that serve as a reminder for you and as a summary to share with anyone who shares a stake in your success.

FOLLOW THE CONTRADICTION

IT'S MONDAY MORNING—That conversation you had with your colleague last Friday still echoes in your mind. As you look at your calendar and start planning the week ahead, you just can't seem to let it go. But after reflecting on things for a minute, you're unable to put your finger on what's bugging you. The phone is already ringing and emails need to be returned, so you move on to other things... The contradiction was right there, alerting you to something that wasn't quite right, but you sped past it. In this example, effective conversations allow us to move forward with a clear mind and a clear sense of what comes next, but when communication gets cloudy, we need to *follow the contradiction*.

BIG IDEAS—The manager's dilemma leaves us feeling trapped, with unwanted options on all sides. This kind of suffocation creates an alignment problem that reduces our capacity to think and act in ways that are consistent with our values and priorities. Once in the manager's dilemma, the fastest way out is to follow the contradiction. Contradictions are those recurring thoughts, uncomfortable feelings, and intuitive hunches that signal trouble ahead. However, if we do not step toward them, they cannot reveal the missing insight.

FIRST STEPS—You follow the contradiction by noticing what's interesting, what stands out, and what doesn't quite fit. Learning to spot contradictions and exercise the patience and discipline required to go wherever they lead offers the seam of daylight you need to move beyond the dilemma. Rather than annoying inconveniences, contradictions become subtle truth tellers that help us sidestep the trouble ahead. To follow a contradiction: (1) pause and spend time reflecting on what it is; (2) break the logical force that causes your knee-jerk reaction to rationalize or move past it; and (3) get third-party insights if you feel turned around and need an objective perspective.

DETERMINE YOUR LINE OF SIGHT

IT'S MONDAY MORNING—When Jill hung up the phone, she was ecstatic. Good news on Monday mornings was rare for her, but the unexpected invitation to take on a new role inside her company was an honor. She had 48 hours to make a decision, and suddenly the obvious choice to say "yes" wasn't so apparent. Was this really the right move for her? Although she was definitely feeling stuck, would a new role change the fundamental reasons why she felt held back? Was there something else to consider that might connect her values, priorities, and goals together in a way that could facilitate the decision-making process? Without a clear *line of sight*, what was good news five minutes earlier now felt like a stressful burden.

BIG IDEAS—Your day has a plan for you, and the dilemma often has a mind of its own. The interruptive demands can disorient you, and when you're turned around, distractions could be opportunities and opportunities could be distractions. Your *line of sight* anchors you amid the clutter and the noise. It is more than just a list of your goals; it's a visible connection among your priorities, desired outcomes, and the factors that influence your pursuit of those things. When others are turned around, chasing their tails, and following shiny objects, you're tethered to a line of sight that sustains focus, direction, and progress toward what matters most even when the dilemma spins you around.

FIRST STEPS—To establish a clear line of sight, respond to these questions: What aspect of my work requires a greater level of focus? Within this area, what are all of the factors that matter to me and to other people that I have to satisfy? Which of these specific factors are important enough to track in my line of sight? If any of these fell away, what impact would that have on the outcomes and goals that this line must produce?

DISTINGUISH YOUR CONTRIBUTION

IT'S MONDAY MORNING—At the weekly meeting, you got "volun-told" to take the lead on a new project. It was your boss who complimented your prior efforts and made it clear that you were the best person to deliver results on this important initiative. He wasn't really asking if you wanted to do it; he was letting you know that you should. But rather than feeling validated for your prior hard work and success, you felt like you just got stuffed inside a small box. This isn't the kind of work you feel passionate about doing, and yet the team—especially your boss—is relying on you to get it done. Only the manager's dilemma can make good news feel so bad.

BIG IDEAS—The manager's dilemma spins our wheels, causing extra efforts with less impact. At the very moment when we need our contributions to the team and organization to be at their best, the dilemma lulls us into thinking that the best way to keep our heads above water is to do a little bit of everything. Rather than saying "yes" to every request, hone in on your distinctive contribution and be selective with the projects and priorities you accept. This move gives you leverage because your impact is clearer and the recognition you receive for doing great work in your area of desired expertise produces more and better opportunities to shine.

FIRST STEPS—To avoid the dilemma's diluted contribution, spend time identifying the key elements of your contribution. Look at the work you do, and then dig deeper to name the *value-added capabilities, vital purpose*, and *relevant results* that are the major elements of your brand. With focused attention, finish these critical statements to jumpstart the process: (1) The strength that I rely upon most during challenging times is...(2) The unique skill/talent I am most proud of is...(3) The subtle impact I make on people and projects is...Over time, contribution-creep caused by the manager's dilemma is eliminated as you answer these questions and distinguish your value.

PLUG THE LEAKS

IT'S MONDAY MORNING—You already feel like the week is getting away from you even though it just began. Instead of the optimistic outlook you hoped for, the pressure is rising and the demands are already piling up. You know you need to move swiftly in order to get it all done, but you don't want to rush either. With phone calls and meetings back-to-back, you realize that this is where your time gets wasted. Generally, each one-hour meeting has about 20 minutes of important discussion. Each 30-minute phone call has about 10 minutes of critical information sharing. However, your day isn't structured around "20s and 10s"; it's built with time-sucking 60s and 30s. The way you inefficiently structure your interactions is *a leak that quietly drains your precious time and energy*. Although you always stay busy, you are anything but 100 percent productive.

BIG IDEAS—The dilemma punches small leaks into our fragile supply of time, energy, resources, and focus. If we fail to notice and address leaks, they silently linger and our neglect requires an even greater effort to repair the leak once additional damage is done. In order to plug the leaks we have to readjust our mindset from reaction to prevention, and then proactively go after them. Ironically, even when we stumble upon a leak, it can lull us into believing that it's okay to ignore it: after all, "it's just a little drip, how bad could it be?" But by the time you square up to face a slow leak, the harm has already been done.

FIRST STEPS—Work is difficult, and we experience a variety of Pings, Dings, and Zings. These diverse leaks frustrate us and block our progress in various ways. To plug them, listen for the drip and follow where it leads. Once you spot the leak: (1) take your time to consider the source; (2) reflect on the causes; (3) get others involved as needed; and (4) take action and then recheck to confirm the patch.

CREATE YOUR CONDITIONS

IT'S MONDAY MORNING—Zach joined a start-up believing that the change of pace from his tenure at an established multinational would give him room to exercise greater autonomy and influence. He delayed major change announcements during his first 90 days so he could get a handle on what was happening, where the talent and good ideas were, and what the obstacles to improvement might be. Recruited with a clear mandate to "shake things up," Zach thought long and hard about what that would look like. Bold ideas, innovative solutions to lingering problems, breakthrough efficiencies—these were all examples of the impact his team would have to make. Staring at a blank white board, the question for Zach was: *What do I need to do right now in order to create an environment where these things can happen.*

BIG IDEAS—The hectic pace of the manager's dilemma make us think things are random, but behind every outcome there is a set of specific conditions that made it possible. Although our conditions powerfully shape our experiences and outcomes, they lie just below the surface so we tend to focus more on the outer achievements we want. As the dilemma causes us to rush and react at the point of experience, we have considerably less influence when things happen in real time. To engineer the outcomes you want, go upstream to the point of possibility.

FIRST STEPS—When we focus on the endpoints of our goals, there is only one path forward. However, when we focus on conditions, we open multiple paths to success. To create conditions, know your goal and then work backward by asking *what has to come first*. This reverse trajectory brings you back to the building blocks of conditions, which include intentional: turns, episodes, and coordinated patterns of interaction that establish the groundwork for what's possible.

FIND THE POCKET OF INFLUENCE

IT'S MONDAY MORNING—Drew couldn't wait any longer. He felt like he was on a treadmill that would never stop so he reasoned that his only choice was to simply jump off. Full of frustration from managing the same difficult client for two years—while being told by his director to "sit tight, new opportunities would likely emerge soon"—Drew was ready to force his boss' hand. Without giving thought to the timing of the conversation, refining his key messages, and clarifying the core request he wanted to make, Drew scheduled the meeting for the only time available on her calendar—6:00 p.m. on Thursday. Although it was clear from the first minute that she was exhausted, Drew pushed on. Not only did the meeting fail to produce the results he wanted, but it went so sideways that Drew likely burned an important bridge in his career.

BIG IDEAS—The dilemma spreads our capacity wafer thin and forces tough choices about how and when we use our limited resources to make an impact. Inside the *pocket of influence*, the conditions and timing are right to use our available energy and effort to influence people and create the outcomes we want. If you can spot these critical moments, you gain leverage to use the pocket of influence to act wisely. Anytime you are knocked out of the pocket, you are subject to the dilemma's wide array of roadblocks and obstacles.

FIRST STEPS—A solid pocket gives you a pivotal moment of pause where your instincts and preparation can positively influence your decision-making. Once you verify the opportunity at hand (i.e., checking for recognition, alignment, timing, and execution), take the leap and make your move. Although the pocket might initially be undefined, you have to confidently step into the space as it develops.

CONVERT CHALLENGES TO FUEL

IT'S MONDAY MORNING—You have managed Tim for a year, and he still doesn't get it. He interacts with colleagues aggressively, which makes him unapproachable and difficult to work with. Your counseling has failed to make a difference in the behavior, but Tim is an effective technical specialist. What he loses from his poor bedside manner, you justify, he more than makes up for with the quality of his procedural work. During a touch point with your supervisor, she asks how things are going with Tim. You say: "*He's doing great, except for the continual blowups he causes within the team.*" Without judgment, your supervisor observes the paradox: "*It seems like you have your head in the sand on this one. In our business, you can't be effective when simple interactions produce the kind of collateral damage that Tim does.*" Her wise words ring true and you come to the conclusion that you've just been avoiding the inevitable.

BIG IDEAS—Managers encounter a constant barrage of barriers to learning and performance that fuel and sustain the dilemma. But these challenges are a form of fuel that can be converted into a vital resource. Identifying and resolving these unavoidable challenges actually flips the scales on the dilemma, which can boost you and your team's performance. When we move toward our barriers, rather than away from them, we get comfortable outside of our comfort zone, and that increases our confidence to respond to all forms of adversity.

FIRST STEPS—Nav-Maps are visual pictures that organize the hidden causes of barriers. At the heart of the tool are four questions you must answer to convert your challenges to fuel: (1) What is the root cause of this challenge? (2) How does it look from various perspectives? (3) What underlying behavior holds the unwanted experience in place? (4) What immediate action can I take to resolve the challenge?

MAKE YOUR GOALS THEIR PRIORITIES

IT'S MONDAY MORNING—A staff member calls you at 8:30 a.m. with urgency in his voice. He tells you that it's important you both find some time to talk face-to-face today. When you meet—to your surprise and disappointment—he explains that he's been unhappy for a while and that he's made the choice to leave for an opportunity outside the organization. Stung, you start to scramble. You're frustrated that you didn't see it coming, and the reality slowly sinks in that the cost of the turnover will make your days that much longer.

BIG IDEAS—When we're stuck in the manager's dilemma, we're unable to be fully present and active in the lives of our team members. This creates blind spots where those Monday morning conversations blindside us. To increase the maximum performance of our people (and reduce the damaging effects of poor performance and turnover), we have to sustain a mutual agenda where individual goals and both team and organizational needs intersect. Managers can help their direct reports establish their agenda, but they also have to "pay themselves first" and create their own.

FIRST STEPS—To help others create their mutual agenda, managers can ask questions about personal goals, and then offer a balance of *expectations* and *support*. This is the necessary mix that enables employees to maximize their investment of time in an organization by defining and pursuing their own long-term career goals while staying true to their team and organization's needs. Likewise, managers can maximize their mutual agenda by clearly and consistently advocating for and accepting the support they need up, down, and across their place on the organization chart. Creating a strong mutual agenda allows you to flip the scales on the dilemma by converting competition into focused alignment and cooperation.

THE FINAL WORD: DID IT WORK?

The greatest measure of effectiveness is the degree to which you can pinpoint positive change. After implementing the recommendations in this book, you should experience shifts like this and be able to recognize that some things are different.

To help you come face-to-face with your dilemma, in chapter 2 I asked you a series of questions in the Presence/Absence test. Flipping a few of those questions inside out, let's assess whether the dilemma's grip has been loosened enough to help you to move out of the *Danger Zone*:

- Do you feel a little less frustrated and a little more satisfied with your work?

- Do you have a little more energy to be productive in the right ways?
- Has the quality and impact of your contribution improved?
- Do you feel a little more confident about your future?

If you can answer "yes" to a few of these questions after reading the book and implementing the concepts, then our time together has been well spent and your manager's dilemma does not stand a chance.

APPENDIX: BLANK NAV-MAP TEMPLATES

CONSTELLATION

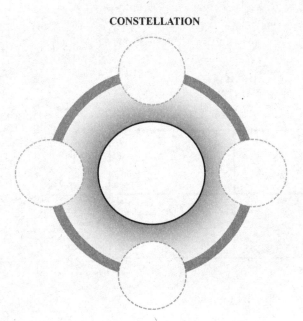

Figure A.1 Constellation template.

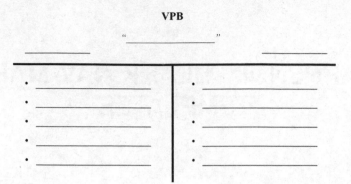

Figure A.2   VPB template.

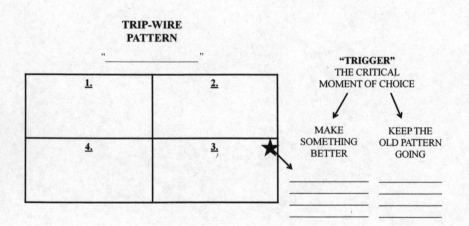

Figure A.3   Trip-wire template.

ACTION
CONTINUUM

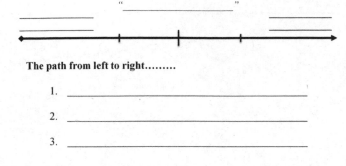

The path from left to right.........

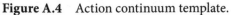

1. _____

2. _____

3. _____

Figure A.4   Action continuum template.

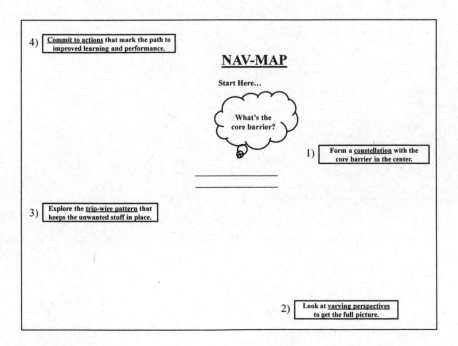

Figure A.5   Nav-Map template.

ABOUT THE AUTHOR

JESSE SOSTRIN, PHD, IS AN INTERNATIONALLY recognized author and thought leader working at the intersection of individual and organizational success. His innovative ideas on leadership and the changing world of work have been featured in a variety of media outlets, including MSNBC, Fox Business, and NPR, and his work has appeared in publications such as *FastCompany, Entrepreneur, Inc., The Huffington Post, The Washington Post, The Chicago Tribune, The Globe & Mail* (Canada), and *The Sun* (United Kingdom). His two previous books, *Re-Making Communication at Work* (2013) and *Beyond the Job Description* (2013), helped to establish his place among the next generation of thinkers challenging the conventional wisdom about working, managing, and leading well. A lifelong learner, Jesse earned academic degrees from Ithaca College, the University of Arizona, and Fielding Graduate University. Outside of his professional life, Jesse's passion is spending time with his family and exploring the natural beauty around their home on the Central Coast of California. Learn more at www.jessesostrin.com and follow him @jessesostrin.

NOTES

PART 1   EMBRACE THE DILEMMA

1. Credit for this analogy goes to my late friend, mentor, and collaborator, Barnett Pearce. We wrote about this concept in our 2009 book: Barnett Pearce, Jesse Sostrin, and Kim Pearce, *CMM Solutions Field Guide for Consultants*, 2nd ed. (San Mateo: Lulu Press, 2011).

INTRODUCTIONS

1. Corporate Executive Board's Executive Guidance for 2013, "Breakthrough Performance in the New Work Environment: Identifying and Enabling the New High Performer," http://www.executiveboard.com/exbd-resources /pdf/executive-guidance/eg2013-annual-final.pdf (accessed October 1, 2014).
2. Ed Frauenheim, "Today's Workforce: Pressed and Stressed," *Workforce*, December 16, 2011, http://www.workforce.com/articles/today-s-workforce -pressed-and-stressed (accessed October 1, 2014).
3. Ibid.
4. Staff Writers, "Lack of Focus Costs Managers both Professionally and Personally," *Red Book Solutions*, January 2011, http://www.bettermanagers .com/pdf/Lack_of_Focus_White_Paper.pdf (accessed October 1, 2014).
5. Theresa M. Welbourne, PhD, and Justin Glen, "Leader Energy and Confidence Ring Alarm Bells," *Leadership Pulse*, June 2014. Referenced on September 11, 2014, at: http://www.eepulse.com/documents/pdfs /EnergyConfidenceDirection.pdf (accessed October 1, 2014).
6. http://www.workforce.com/articles/today-s-workforce-pressed-and -stressed (accessed October 1, 2014).
7. Corporate Executive Board's Executive Guidance for 2013, "Breakthrough Performance in the New Work Environment."

8. Corporate Executive Board, "CLC Learning and Development High Performance 2012 Survey," 2; "CLC Performance Management 2002 Survey," and Corporate Executive Board's CLC Organizational 2008 Redesign Survey, http://www.executiveboard.com/exbd-resources/pdf /executive-guidance/eg2013-annual-final.pdf (accessed October 1, 2014).

9. If you want see the glass as half full in this statistic, you might be tempted to interpret the increase in headcount as a positive trend, suggesting that organizations are flatter now and managers actually have more self-directed human capital to meet the demand. However, that interpretation fails to take into account the structural cutbacks and systemic reductions that organizations have made across the board.

10. Randall Beck and Jim Harter, *Gallup Business Journal*, March 2014, "Why Great Managers Are So Rare," http://www.gallup.com /businessjournal/167975/why-great-managers-rare.aspx (accessed April 2, 2014).

11. Harry Levinson, "When Executives Burn Out," *Harvard Business Review*, September 12, 2014, http://hbr.org/1996/07/when-executives -burn-out/ar/1 (accessed September 13, 2014).

12. Katherine Milkman, "Why Fresh Starts Matter," *Strategy & Business*, August 8, 2014.

13. I owe a debt of gratitude to a few influential thinkers whose research and writing have influenced my work on these concepts. Kurt Lewin, the renowned psychologist, developed his *force field analysis*, which demonstrated that the best way to resolve a force that blocked change was to simultaneously reduce the resistance and the cause. Chris Argyris, the seminal Harvard Business School professor, developed his concept of *double-loop learning*, which demonstrates the importance of resolving root cause issues that hold the deeper learning and performance barriers in place. And finally, Wendell Berry, the poet and ecological pioneer, wrote about the concept of *solving for pattern*, which means any systemic solution has to address multiple issues simultaneously. These concepts gave me the inspiration to develop solutions to the manager's dilemma that turn its double negative into a positive.

1   THE EVOLUTION OF A DILEMMA

1. Harry Levinson, "When Executives Burn Out," *Harvard Business Review*, 1981, http://hbr.org/1996/07/when-executives-burn-out/ar/1 (accessed September 12, 2014).
2. These factors were excerpted from: Mayo Clinic Staff, "Job Burnout: How to Spot It and Take Action," http://www.mayoclinic.org/healthy-living/adult-health/in-depth/burnout/art-20046642 (accessed on September 12, 2014).
3. Howard McClusky, "Education for Aging: The Scope of the Field and Perspectives for the Future," in *Learning for Aging*, eds. S. Grabowski and W. D. Mason (Washington, DC: Adult Education Association of the USA, 1974), 324–355.
4. Peter Vaill, *Learning as a Way of Being* (San Francisco, CA: Jossey-Bass, 1996), 15.
5. Don Marrs has told his complete story in his fantastic book *Executive in Passage: When Life Lets You Know It's Time to Change, Let That Knowing Lead You* (Santa Monica, CA: Barrington Sky Publishing, 1990).

2   KNOW YOUR DILEMMA?

1. The effects of the manager's dilemma often resemble typical patterns of active and passive disengagement. When a manager experiences these effects, they have a compounding impact on the manager's portfolio of work, as well as on his direct reports. For a good summary of classic disengagement outcomes, see Nikki Blacksmith and Jim Harter, "Majority of American Workers Not Engaged in Their Jobs," *Gallup Wellbeing*, October 28, 2011, http://www.gallup.com/poll/150383/majority-american-workers-not-engaged-jobs.aspx (accessed on April 18, 2013).
2. Howard McClusky, "Course of the Adult Life Span," in *Psychology of Adults*, ed. W. C. Hallenbeck (Chicago: Adult Education Association of USA), 1963.
3. Peter Vaill, *Learning as a Way of Being: Strategies for Survival in a World of Permanent White Water* (San Francisco, CA: Jossey-Bass, 1996).
4. Stanford professor Carol Dweck points out that we have one of two mindsets: growth or fixed. These prevailing mindsets are associated with more

complex patterns of thought and action and they dictate what is possible in our response to challenge situations and subtle forms of adversity. As it relates to the manager's dilemma, two of the most common responses (hero and evader) are growth-driven. The other two (survivor and deserter) are fixed to the assumption that it doesn't matter because things cannot change.

3   FOLLOW THE CONTRADICTION

1. Scott Plous, *The Psychology of Judgment and Decision Making* (New York: McGraw-Hill, 1993).
2. Kingsley Davis, *Human Society* (New York: Macmillan, 1942).
3. Jesse Sostrin, *Beyond the Job Description: How Managers and Employees Can Navigate the True Demands of the Job* (New York: Palgrave Macmillan, 2013).
4. The phrase "hidden curriculum of work" is a trademark of Jesse Sostrin. For formatting reasons, the phrase is referred to throughout the book simply as "the hidden curriculum of work."
5. Jesse Sostrin, *Re-Making Communication at Work* (New York: Palgrave Macmillan, 2013).

4   DETERMINE YOUR LINE OF SIGHT

1. Jerry Gilley and Ann Maycunich, *Beyond the Learning Organization* (New York: Perseus Books, 2000).
2. Chris Argyris, *Overcoming Organizational Defense. Facilitating Organizational Learning* (Boston: Allyn and Bacon, 1990).
3. Antoine de Saint-Exupery, *The Wisdom of the Sands* (University of Chicago Press, 1979)
4. Alain de Botton, "A Kinder, Gentler Philosophy of Success," http://www.ted.com/talks/alain_de_botton_a_kinder_gentler_philosophy_of_success.html (accessed on January 7, 2013).
5. Hugh MacLeod, *Ignore Everybody: And 39 Other Keys to Creativity* (New York: Penguin Group, 2009).

5   DISTINGUISH YOUR CONTRIBUTION

1.. I originally published this career development framework in my previous book, *Beyond the Job Description*. It includes more detailed ways to establish a "Future-Proof Plan" that gives you constructive methods for creating the working life you want. For more information, see Jesse Sostrin, *Beyond the Job Description: How Managers and Employees Can Navigate the True Demands of the Job* (New York: Palgrave Macmillan, 2013).

6 PLUG THE LEAKS

1. Paula Caproni, *Management Skills for Everyday Life* (Upper Saddle River, NJ: Pearson, 2005).
2. Martin Covington, *Making the Grade: A Self-Worth Perspective on Motivation and School Reform* (Cambridge, England: Cambridge University Press, 1992).
3. Jeffrey Pfeffer and Robert Sutton, *The Knowing-Doing Gap: How Smart Companies Turn Knowledge into Action* (Boston, MA: Harvard Business School Publishing, 2000).

7 CREATE YOUR CONDITIONS

1. Stephen Covey, A. Roger Merrill, and Rebecca R. Merrill, *First Things First: To Live, to Love, to Learn, to Leave a Legacy* (New York: Simon and Schuster, 1994).
2. David Allen, *Getting Things Done: The Art of Stress-Free Productivity* (New York: Penguin Books, 2001).
3. Greg McKeown, *Essentialism: The Disciplined Pursuit of Less* (New York: Crown Business, 2014).

9 CONVERT CHALLENGES TO FUEL

1. Kevin Ford and James Osterhaus, *The Thing in the Bushes: Turning Organizational Blind Spots into Competitive Advantage* (Colorado Springs, CO: Pinon Press, 2001).
2. This system was developed through years of rigorous research and practice. The process of making Nav-Maps and resolving workplace challenges in this way was most recently published in my book, *Beyond the Job Description*. There are chapters devoted to the origins of the process, including the research methodology, as well as how individual contributors and leaders can apply it. Jesse Sostrin, *Beyond the Job Description: How*

Managers and Employees Can Navigate the True Demands of the Job (New York: Palgrave Macmillan, 2013).

3. These hierarchical and facilitative characteristics were developed over the years by my former colleagues at the Institute of Cultural Affairs.

10   MAKE YOUR GOALS THEIR PRIORITIES

1. The catchphrase "free agent" has been used in a variety of contexts. I believe it was first coined by the influential author and former speech writer Daniel Pink. See his *A Whole New Mind: Moving from the Information Age to the Conceptual Age* (New York: Riverhead Books, 2005).

2. Jack Wiley, "Business Success Depends on Good Managers," *HR Magazine*, December 3, 2009, http://www.hrmagazine.co.uk/hro/analysis/1016196 /business-success-depends-managers (accessed October 14, 2014).

3. "Breakthrough Performance in the New Work Environment: Identifying and Enabling the New High Performer," from Corporate Executive Board's Executive Guidance for 2013, http://www.executiveboard.com /exbd-resources/pdf/executive-guidance/eg2013-annual-final.pdf(accessed October 25, 2014).

BIBLIOGRAPHY

Berry, Wendell. *Solving for Pattern*—Chapter 9 in *The Gift of Good Land: Further Essays Cultural & Agricultural*. North Point Press, 1981. Originally published in the Rodale Press periodical *The New Farm*.

Davis, Kingsley. *Human Society*. New York: Macmillan, 1942.

Deal, Terrence and Kennedy, Allan. *Corporate Cultures: The Rites and Rituals of Corporate Life*. Harmondsworth: Penguin Books, 1982.

Drucker, Peter. *Post-Capitalist Society*. New York: HarperCollins, 1993.

Few, Steven. *Now You See It: Simple Visualization Techniques for Quantitative Analysis*. Oakland: Analytics Press, 2009.

Ford, Kevin and Osterhaus, James. *The Thing in the Bushes: Turning Organizational Blind Spots into Competitive Advantage*. Colorado Springs: Pinon Press, 2001.

Gilley, Jerry and Maycunich, Ann. *Beyond the Learning Organization*. New York: Perseus Books, 2000.

Hall, Doug. *Careers in Organizations*. Glenview: Goodyear Publishing, 1976.

Howard, Ann, *The Changing Nature of Work*. San Francisco: Jossey-Bass, 1995.

Jablin, Fredric. "Organizational Entry, Assimilation, and Exit." In *Handbook of Organizational Communication*, edited by Fredric Jablin, Linda Putnam, K. Roberts, and L. W. Porter, 679–740. Newbury Park: Sage Publications, 1987.

Katz, Daniel and Kahn, Robert. *The Social Psychology of Organizations*. New York: John Wiley & Sons, 1978.

Kayser, Thomas. *Mining Group Gold: How to Cash in on the Collaborative Brain Power of a Group*. El Segundo: Serif Publishing, 1990.

Kegan, Robert. *In Over Our Heads: The Mental Demands of Modern Life*. Cambridge: Harvard University Press, 1994.

Lewin, Kurt. *Field Theory and Social Science.* New York: Harper, 1951.

McClusky, Howard. "Education for Aging: The Scope of the Field and Perspectives for the Future." In *Learning for Aging,* edited by Stanley Grabowski and Dean Mason, 324–355. Washington, DC: Adult Education Association of the USA, 1974.

Peters, Tom. *Thriving on Chaos: Handbook for a Managerial Revolution.* New Jersey: Macmillan, 1987.

Pink, Daniel. A *Whole New Mind: Moving from the Information Age to the Conceptual Age.* New York: Riverhead Books, 2005.

Sostrin, Jesse. *Beyond the Job Description: How Managers and Employees Can Navigate the True Demands of the Job.* New York: Palgrave Macmillan, 2013.

———. *Re-Making Communication at Work.* New York: Palgrave Macmillan, 2013.

Vaill, Peter. *Learning as a Way of Being.* San Francisco: Jossey-Bass, 1996.

INDEX